Rust Programming Language for Operating Systems

Build Secure and High-Performance Operating Systems in Rust

Jeff Stuart

1

Discover Other Books in the Series

"Rust Programming Language for Beginners: The Ultimate Beginner's Guide to Safe and Fast Programming"

"Rust Programming language for Network: Build Fast, Secure, and Scalable Systems"

"Rust Programming Language for Web Assembly: Build Blazing-Fast, Next-Gen Web Applications"

"Rust Programming Language for Web Development: Building High-Performance Web Applications and APIs"

"Rust Programming Language for Blockchains: Build Secure, Scalable, and High-Performance Distributed Systems"

"Rust Programming Language for Cybersecurity: Writing Secure Code to Implementing Advanced Cryptographic Solutions"

"Rust Programming Language for IoT: The Complete Guide to Developing Secure and Efficient Smart Devices"

"Rust programming Language for Artificial Intelligence: High-performance machine learning with unmatched speed, memory safety, and concurrency from AI innovation"

Disclaimer

The information provided in *"**Rust Programming Language for Operating Systems**: Build Secure and High-Performance Operating Systems in Rust"* by Jeff Stuart is intended solely for educational and informational purposes.

Readers are encouraged to consult qualified professionals or official documentation for specific technical, legal, or professional guidance related to their projects.

Introduction

Welcome to "**Rust Programming Language for Operating Systems: Construct Secure and High-Performance Operating Systems in Rust**." In a time when the need for secure and efficient software is unprecedented, the Rust programming language has emerged as an essential resource for system developers. This book is designed to navigate you through the complexities of utilizing Rust to create operating systems that not only fulfill but surpass the stringent demands of performance and security.

Operating systems serve as the foundation of computing, managing everything from file operations to resource distribution and user engagement. As technology progresses, the challenges related to system vulnerabilities and performance limitations also increase. Conventional programming languages frequently struggle to achieve a balance between safety and efficiency, resulting in bugs and security vulnerabilities. Rust, with its focus on memory safety, concurrency, and zero-cost abstractions, offers a contemporary framework to effectively address these issues. In this comprehensive guide, we will explore the fundamental concepts of operating system design and development with a focus on Rust. You'll learn about:

Memory Management: Understand how Rust's ownership model can prevent common pitfalls associated with memory leaks and race conditions.

Concurrency: Discover how to leverage Rust's concurrency features to build responsive and efficient systems.

Modules and Kernel Development: Get hands-on experience creating kernel modules that communicate seamlessly with hardware and other software components.

Security Best Practices: Implement robust security measures using Rust's powerful type system and features that eliminate whole classes of vulnerabilities.

Performance Optimization: Learn strategies to optimize your operating systems for maximum efficiency and speed.

Whether you're a seasoned developer seeking to expand your toolkit or a newcomer looking to dive into the realm of operating system development, this book caters to various levels of expertise. Each chapter will provide practical examples, insightful explanations, and exercises designed to solidify your understanding of the concepts discussed.

Throughout this journey, you will be challenged to think critically about design choices, while also being encouraged to experiment and push the boundaries of what is possible in Rust.

We invite you to join us as we embark on a comprehensive exploration of building secure and high- performance operating systems with Rust. Equip yourself with the knowledge and skills to contribute to the next generation of software that stands strong against the evolving landscape of computing challenges.

Chapter 1: Introduction to Rust for Systems Programming

Systems programming, a field that lies at the convergence of hardware and software, necessitates the use of languages that facilitate direct interaction with memory and hardware while maintaining reliability and safety. Among the languages crafted to fulfill these requirements, Rust has emerged as a leading candidate, positioned to transform the landscape of systems programming.

1.1 What is Rust?

Rust is a systems programming language that emphasizes both performance and safety, particularly in the context of safe concurrency. Developed by Mozilla Research, Rust provides low-level control similar to that of C and C++, while integrating contemporary programming paradigms that mitigate some of the traditional challenges associated with these languages, such as buffer overflows and null pointer dereferences. The syntax of Rust is shaped by a blend of functional and imperative programming styles, rendering it both familiar and unique.

A fundamental principle of Rust is to enable developers to create safe and concurrent systems with minimal performance overhead. This is accomplished through its groundbreaking ownership model, which imposes stringent regulations on memory access and sharing across threads. By utilizing compile-time checks, Rust significantly diminishes the likelihood of runtime errors, thereby bolstering the robustness of software.

1.2 The Need for Systems Programming

Systems programming serves as the backbone of modern

computing infrastructures. It encompasses the development of operating systems, device drivers, embedded systems, and performance-critical applications. With the proliferation of complex hardware architectures and the demand for high-performance computing, there is an imperative need for a language that can bridge the traditional low-level programming capabilities with contemporary software engineering practices.

1.2.1 Efficiency and Performance

In systems programming, performance is a non-negotiable trait. Code must run efficiently, maximizing CPU and memory usage while providing capabilities to manage resources effectively. Rust's zero-cost abstractions mean that developers can write high-level code without incurring penalties at runtime.

Optimizations performed by the Rust compiler ensure that the resulting binaries are as efficient as those written in languages like C or C++.

1.2.2 Safety and Concurrency

As systems grow in complexity, so does the challenge of ensuring safety, particularly in concurrent programming. Traditional languages like C often leave memory management and concurrency in the hands of the developer, leading to vulnerabilities and undefined behavior. Rust, however, enforces safety through its ownership system, which ensures data race freedom and memory safety without needing a garbage collector, making it suitable for concurrent programming environments.

1.3 Key Features of Rust

To appreciate Rust's place in systems programming, it's essential to understand some of its standout features: ### 1.3.1 Ownership and Borrowing Rust introduces a unique ownership model that ensures each piece of data has a single owner at any point in time. This model is complemented by the concepts of borrowing and lifetimes, which allow functions to access data without taking ownership. This structure eliminates common memory issues found in other languages, such as double-free errors and memory leaks.

1.3.2 Concurrency Without Fear

Rust's approach to concurrency is both powerful and intuitive. With its ownership model, the language ensures that data is either mutable or immutable but never both at the same time, effectively preventing data races during concurrent access. This means developers can write multithreaded applications confidently, knowing that the compiler will catch potential issues at compile time.

1.3.3 Comprehensive Tooling

Rust's ecosystem is built around a robust set of tools that enhance the development experience. The package manager, Cargo, simplifies dependency management and project setup, while Clippy and Rustfmt help maintain code quality and consistency. Rust's built-in support for unit testing also encourages developers to write reliable and maintainable code.

1.4 The Ecosystem and Community

One of the strongest aspects of Rust is its vibrant and growing community. The Rust community prides itself on inclusiveness and collaboration, fostering an environment where developers of all skill levels can contribute to and learn from the language and its ecosystem. This community-driven approach has led to the rapid evolution of libraries and tools that extend Rust's capabilities far beyond the core language — from web development to embedded systems.

With its unique features and a strong community backing, Rust is not just a tool for systems programmers; it is a paradigm shift that encourages developers to rethink how they write software that interacts with hardware.

The Benefits of Rust in Low-Level Programming

Traditionally, languages like C and C++ have dominated this field due to their performance and close-to-the-metal capabilities. However, over the past decade, Rust has emerged as a powerful alternative, bringing a host of advantages that address some of the long-standing issues associated with low-level programming.

This chapter explores the key benefits of Rust in this domain, illustrating how it modernizes and improves the development process.

1. Memory Safety without Garbage Collection

One of the most significant benefits of Rust is its emphasis on memory safety without the need for garbage collection. In low-level programming, developers often manage memory manually, which can lead to a variety of bugs, including use-after-free errors, dangling pointers, and buffer overflows. These issues not only compromise security but can also lead to unpredictable behavior in applications.

Rust employs a unique ownership model, where every piece of memory has a single owner, and when the owner goes out of scope, the memory is automatically reclaimed. This model prevents data races and ensures that developers do not need to worry about the lifecycle of their resources, unlike in C or C++. Moreover, Rust's borrowing system enables developers to check at compile time whether references to data are valid, effectively eliminating many common memory-related bugs before a program ever runs.

2. Concurrency Without Fear

Concurrency is an essential aspect of modern programming, allowing developers to take advantage of multi- core processors to improve performance. However, concurrent programming has traditionally been fraught with dangers, including race conditions, deadlocks, and other synchronization issues that can be difficult to diagnose and fix.

Rust's design promotes safe concurrency. The language's ownership and borrowing principles extend to the concurrent context, ensuring that data cannot be mutated unexpectedly while being accessed from multiple threads. The Rust compiler enforces these rules at compile time, allowing developers to write concurrent code that is both efficient and safe. This results in fewer bugs and a more straightforward debugging process, enabling developers to build robust systems without the worry of subtle threading issues.

3. Performance with Zero-Cost Abstractions

One of the most critical considerations in low-level programming is performance. Developers want their programs to run as efficiently as possible, especially when interfacing directly with hardware. Rust provides performance on par with C and C++ while offering higher-level abstractions that do not compromise on speed.

The concept of "zero-cost abstractions" is central to Rust's philosophy. This means that when developers use abstractions in Rust, they pay no additional runtime cost compared to hand-written low-level code. The Rust compiler performs advanced optimizations, allowing developers to write cleaner, more maintainable code without sacrificing performance. This leads to an increase in productivity, as developers can spend less time managing low-level details and more time focusing on solving higher-level problems.

4. Enhanced Tooling and Ecosystem

Rust features a modern tooling ecosystem that significantly enhances the low-level programming experience. The Rust package manager, Cargo, simplifies dependency management, making it easy to include libraries and frameworks. The ecosystem is enriched with numerous high-quality crates (Rust libraries) that can be leveraged in various projects, from embedded systems to operating systems.

Furthermore, Rust's documentation and community support are robust and welcoming. Comprehensive and clear documentation, along with active community forums, enable developers to quickly find solutions to challenges they encounter. This collaborative spirit fosters a helpful environment for both newcomers and experienced developers alike.

5. Strong Community and Industry Adoption

The Rust community is known for being inclusive, supportive, and focused on fostering good practices in programming. Its governance promotes transparency and collaboration, ensuring that the language and its ecosystem continue to evolve in a way that benefits developers.

Additionally, Rust has seen growing adoption in industry sectors that require high performance and safety, such as finance, telecommunications, and even game development. Companies like Mozilla, Microsoft, and Amazon are embracing Rust for its ability to reduce bugs and enhance security in their systems. This momentum is indicative of wider recognition of Rust's benefits in low-level programming, further driving its development and improvement.

By leveraging Rust, developers can create more reliable, efficient, and maintainable systems, paving the way for the next generation of software development. In an era where software security and performance are paramount, the adoption of Rust may not just be beneficial—it may be essential.

Setting Up Your Rust Development Environment

However, to harness the power of Rust, you first need to set up a conducive development environment. This chapter will guide you through the necessary steps to install Rust, configure your development tools, and create your first Rust project.

1. Installing Rust ### 1.1 Prerequisites

Before diving into the installation, ensure your system meets the following requirements:

Operating System: Rust can be installed on Windows, macOS, and various Linux distributions. Ensure your OS is up-to-date.

Command Line Interface: Familiarity with the terminal or command prompt is helpful as you'll be using it for most installations and commands.

1.2 Installing Rust using rustup

The recommended way to install Rust is through `rustup`, an installer for the Rust programming language.

`rustup` manages Rust versions and associated tools efficiently. Follow these steps:

Open your terminal (Command Prompt, PowerShell, or Terminal).

Run the following command to download and install `rustup`:

For **Unix-based systems** (Linux, macOS):

```bash
curl --proto '=https' --tlsv1.2 -sSf https://sh.rustup.rs | sh
```

For **Windows**:

```bash
```

iwr https://sh.rustup.rs -useb | iex
```

**Follow the on-screen instructions**. You may be prompted to adjust your path variable, which ensures that Rust is accessible from your command line.

**Close and reopen your terminal** or run `source $HOME/.cargo/env` (for Unix-based systems) to ensure the changes take effect.

### 1.3 Verifying the Installation

To confirm that Rust is installed correctly, run the following command:

```bash

rustc --version
```

This command should return the version of Rust you installed. Additionally, `cargo`, Rust's package manager and build system, can also be verified:

```bash

cargo --version
```

If both commands return version numbers, you're ready to start coding! ## 2. Setting Up an Integrated Development Environment (IDE)

While you can use any text editor to write Rust code, an IDE that supports Rust can greatly enhance your
```

productivity. Below are some popular options and how to set them up.

2.1 Visual Studio Code (VSCode)

Download and Install VSCode from [the official website](https://code.visualstudio.com/).

Install Rust Analyzer:

Open VSCode.

Go to the Extensions view by clicking on the Extensions icon in the Activity Bar on the side or using the shortcut `Ctrl+Shift+X`.

Search for "Rust Analyzer" and click "Install". ### 2.2 IntelliJ IDEA with the Rust Plugin

Download and Install IntelliJ IDEA from [the JetBrains website](https://www.jetbrains.com/idea/).

Install the Rust Plugin:

Open IntelliJ IDEA and go to `Preferences` (or `Settings` on Windows).

Select `Plugins`, then search for "Rust" and click "Install". ## 3. Creating Your First Rust Project

With Rust installed and your IDE set up, it's time to create your first Rust project. ### 3.1 Using Cargo to Create a New Project

Open your terminal.

Navigate to the directory where you want to create your Rust project. For example:

```bash
```

```
cd ~/Projects
```

Run the following command to create a new project named `hello_world`:

```bash
cargo new hello_world
```

Navigate into the project directory:

```bash
cd hello_world
```

3.2 Understanding the Project Structure

Once you create a project, `cargo` sets up a directory structure:

```
hello_world/
Cargo.toml    # Package configuration file src
main.rs       # Main source file
```

Cargo.toml: This file contains metadata about your project and its dependencies.

src/main.rs: This is where your Rust code will go. It contains a basic "Hello, World!" program by default.

3.3 Building and Running Your Project

To build and run your project, use the following command in your project directory:

```bash
cargo run
```

You should see the output:

```

```

Hello, world!

```

```

Congratulations! You have set up your Rust development environment and created your first Rust program. ## 4. Additional Tools

To further enhance your Rust development experience, consider installing the following tools:

Rustfmt: Formats your Rust code.

```bash
rustup component add rustfmt
```

Clippy: A linter for Rust, which helps catch common mistakes and improve your code.

```bash
rustup component add clippy
```

Visual debugging tools: Many IDEs offer plugins and tools to help debug Rust applications easily.

Setting up your Rust development environment is a

straightforward process that involves installing Rust, selecting an appropriate IDE, and creating a new Rust project. With this foundation, you can explore more advanced Rust features and build powerful applications. In the following chapters, we'll delve deeper into the Rust language, build projects, and learn more about best practices for writing efficient and safe code. Happy coding!

Chapter 2: Rust Fundamentals for Operating Systems

This chapter presents the essential principles of Rust that are vital for developing resilient operating systems. We will examine key elements, ranging from data types to ownership concepts, that establish Rust as a preferred option for systems-level programming.

2.1 Overview of Rust

Rust is a systems programming language created by Mozilla, focusing on performance and safety, especially in terms of safe concurrency. Its design philosophy supports low-level programming while incorporating contemporary language features that improve developer efficiency. Rust is organized, strongly typed, and ensures memory safety without relying on a garbage collector.### 2.1.1 Key Features of Rust

Memory Safety: Rust employs a unique ownership system to manage memory allocation without the risk of leaks or dangling pointers.

Zero-Cost Abstractions: High-level constructs in Rust do not impose additional runtime overhead, making it suitable for OS development.

Concurrency: Rust's type system and ownership model help prevent data races, making concurrent programming more manageable and safe.

Pattern Matching: The robust pattern matching capabilities in Rust simplify control flow, allowing powerful and expressive data handling.

Error Handling: Through the use of `Result` and

`Option` types, Rust provides a systematic approach to error management, enhancing reliability.

2.2 Basic Syntax and Data Types

Before diving deeper into Rust's programming paradigms, it's essential to understand its syntax and basic data types.

2.2.1 Variables and Data Types

Rust is statically typed, meaning that variable types are resolved at compile time. The primary data types in Rust include:

Scalar Types: Including integers (`i32`, `u32`), floating points (`f32`, `f64`), booleans (`bool`), and characters (`char`).

Compound Types: Such as tuples and arrays. Tuples can hold mixed data types, while arrays are fixed size and homogeneous.

Example:

```rust
let x: i32 = 5;
let y: f64 = 3.14; let z: char = 'A';
let tuple: (i32, f64) = (42, 3.14);
let array: [i32; 5] = [1, 2, 3, 4, 5];
```

2.2.2 Control Flow

Rust features standard control flow constructs including `if`, `loop`, `while`, and `for`.

Example:

```rust
for number in 1..5 { println!("{}", number);
}
```

2.3 Ownership, Borrowing, and Lifetimes

Rust's ownership model is arguably the most distinctive feature separating it from other programming languages. Understanding ownership, borrowing, and lifetimes is crucial for writing safe and efficient systems code.

2.3.1 Ownership

Each value in Rust has a single owner, which is the variable that holds it. When the owner goes out of scope, the value is automatically dropped, preventing memory leaks.

Example:

```rust
{
let s = String::from("Hello");
} // s is dropped here
```

2.3.2 Borrowing

Rust allows references to values without taking ownership, enabling safe sharing of data. Borrowing can be mutable

24

or immutable:

Immutable Borrowing: Allows multiple immutable references to be created.

Mutable Borrowing: Allows one mutable reference, preventing data races.

Example:

```rust
let s1 = String::from("hello");

let s2 = &s1; // immutable borrow
```

2.3.3 Lifetimes

Lifetimes are Rust's way of ensuring that references are valid as long as the data they point to exists. By annotating lifetimes, developers can express the scope of references, thus preventing dangling references.

Example:

```rust
fn longest<'a>(s1: &'a str, s2: &'a str) -> &'a str { if s1.len() > s2.len() {

s1

} else { s2

}

}
```

2.4 Structs and Enums

Rust's custom data types, such as structs and enums, allow developers to create complex systems. ### 2.4.1 Structs

Structs are used to create custom data types by grouping multiple related values.

Example:

```rust
struct Process { id: u32, name: String,
}
```

2.4.2 Enums

Enums provide a way to define a type that can take on one of several variants, making them powerful for modeling states or distinct data.

Example:

```rust
enum State { Running, Suspended, Terminated,
}
```

2.5 Concurrency in Rust

Concurrency is essential in an operating system, where multiple tasks run simultaneously. Rust's concurrency model uses ownership to avoid common pitfalls like data races.

2.5.1 Threads

Rust's standard library provides thread support, allowing the creation of lightweight concurrent tasks.

Example:

```rust
use std::thread;

let handle = thread::spawn(|| { println!("Hello from a thread!");
});

handle.join().unwrap(); // Wait for the thread to finish
```

2.5.2 Message Passing

Rust encourages communication between threads through message passing, using channels to send data safely.

Example:

```rust
use std::sync::mpsc;

let (tx, rx) = mpsc::channel();

let handle = thread::spawn(move || {
tx.send("Hello").unwrap();
});

println!("{}", rx.recv().unwrap()); // Receives the message
```

Understanding the fundamentals discussed in this chapter — ownership, borrowing, data types, and concurrency — lays a solid foundation for building reliable operating systems. The subsequent chapters will expand on these concepts, demonstrating how to apply Rust fundamentals in real-world OS design and development.

27

Ownership, Borrowing, and Lifetimes in Depth

Key to its design are the concepts of ownership, borrowing, and lifetimes—mechanisms that enforce memory safety and manage resources efficiently. This chapter delves into these concepts in detail, exploring how they apply to operating system development, where resource management is critical.

1. Ownership

1.1 The Ownership Model

At the core of Rust's memory management is the ownership model. In Rust, every piece of data has a single owner, which is typically a variable. When the owner of a piece of data goes out of scope, Rust automatically deallocates that data, ensuring there are no memory leaks.

Example:

```rust
fn main() {

let x = String::from("Hello, Rust!"); println!("{}", x); // x owns the String

} // x goes out of scope and the memory is freed
```

1.2 Transferring Ownership

Ownership can be transferred from one variable to another, a process known as "moving." When a variable is moved, the previous owner can no longer be used, preventing dangling references.

Example:

```rust
fn main() {
let s1 = String::from("Hello");
let s2 = s1; // s1's ownership is moved to s2 println!("{}", s2); // Valid
// println!("{}", s1); // Invalid: s1 is no longer valid
}
```

In operating systems, this ownership model is useful for managing resources such as memory buffers, file handles, and system states, reducing the risks of memory corruption and leaks.

2. Borrowing

2.1 Borrowing Basics

Instead of transferring ownership, Rust allows you to "borrow" data. Borrowing comes in two flavors: mutable and immutable. An immutable borrow allows read access, while a mutable borrow allows changes to the borrowed data.

Immutable Borrowing

```rust
fn main() {
let s = String::from("Hello");
let len = get_length(&s); // s is borrowed immutably println!("Length: {}", len);
```

```
}
fn get_length(s: &String) -> usize { s.len() // Immutable
borrow is allowed
}
```

Mutable Borrowing

```rust
fn main() {
let mut s = String::from("Hello"); change(&mut s); // s is
borrowed mutably println!("{}", s);
}
fn change(s: &mut String) {
s.push_str(", Rust!"); // Mutable borrow allows changes
}
```

2.2 Borrowing Rules

There are strict rules governing borrowing:

You can have multiple immutable borrows (`&T`) of data at the same time.

Or you can have one mutable borrow (`&mut T`), but not both mutable and immutable borrows at the same time.

These rules prevent data races and ensure thread safety, crucial in systems programming where concurrency is commonplace.

3. Lifetimes

3.1 Understanding Lifetimes

Lifetimes in Rust are a way of expressing the scope during which a reference is valid. A lifetime tells the Rust compiler how long references should be valid.

In many cases, Rust infers lifetimes automatically, but sometimes explicit annotations are required. #### Example:

```rust
fn longest<'a>(s1: &'a str, s2: &'a str) -> &'a str { if s1.len() > s2.len() {

s1

} else { s2

}

}
```

In this example, the function `longest` indicates that the returned reference will be valid for as long as both input references are valid. This avoids dangling references that can occur in systems programming.

3.2 Lifetime Annotations

Life in the operating system can be complex with various subsystems and components interacting. Lifetime annotations enable safe interaction among concurrent components by ensuring that references do not outlive the data they point to.

Static Lifetime: Data that lives for the entire duration of the program.

Non-static Lifetime: Scoped data, determined by lexical scope. ### 3.3 Lifetime Elision

Rust uses lifetime elision rules to streamline function signatures and make them easier to understand. For instance, the compiler will infer lifetimes based on the function's parameters and return type, reducing boilerplate code.

4. Applications in Operating Systems ### 4.1 Memory Safety

In operating systems, where direct hardware interaction and resource allocation occur, the ownership and borrowing rules of Rust help prevent many common bugs, such as buffer overflows, use-after-free, and double frees.

4.2 Concurrency

As operating systems inherently manage concurrent processes, Rust's borrowing rules facilitate safe concurrency. With the guarantee that data races cannot occur, as long as shared data obeys the borrowing rules, developers can confidently implement multi-threaded operations.

4.3 Resource Management

Rust's ownership model simplifies resource management in operating systems, allowing developers to define clear lifetimes for resources like file descriptors. This enables automatic cleanup without requiring a garbage collector, making it ideal for the performance-critical environments characteristic of systems programming.

Understanding ownership, borrowing, and lifetimes is essential for leveraging the full power of Rust in operating systems development. These concepts provide a robust framework for memory management and resource handling, which are critical for building reliable and efficient systems. As Rust continues to gain traction in systems programming, mastering these principles will be fundamental for developers looking to harness its capabilities.

Essential Rust Data Structures for Systems Programming

In this chapter, we will explore some essential Rust data structures that are particularly valuable in systems programming contexts, providing insights into their characteristics, use cases, and performance considerations.

1. Basic Data Types

To effectively utilize more complex data structures, it is crucial to understand Rust's basic data types. Rust supports several primitive types, including:

- **Integers**: `i32`, `u32`, `i64`, `u64`, etc.

Floating-Point Numbers: `f32`, `f64`

Characters: `char`

Booleans: `bool`

These types allow developers to handle numerical computations, boolean logic, and textual data, forming the foundational building blocks for larger structures.

2. Arrays and Slices ### 2.1 Arrays

Arrays in Rust are fixed-size collections of elements of the same type. Their size must be known at compile time, offering reliable memory access and performance. For example:

```rust
let numbers: [i32; 5] = [1, 2, 3, 4, 5];
```

2.2 Slices

Unlike arrays, slices are dynamically-sized views into contiguous sequences of elements. Slices provide a more flexible way to handle collections while still being efficient. They do not own the data they reference but provide access to it:

```rust
let slice: &[i32] = &numbers[1..4]; // This references a portion of the array
```

3. Vectors

Vectors (`Vec<T>`) are dynamic, growable arrays. They are one of the most commonly used data structures in Rust for systems programming. Vectors manage their own memory and automatically resize as elements are added or removed:

```rust
let mut vec: Vec<i32> = Vec::new(); vec.push(1);
vec.push(2);
```

Performance Consideration

Vectors ensure efficient memory management due to their internal structure, which uses a contiguous block of memory and allows for O(1) access time. However, care must be taken when resizing because this sometimes involves reallocating memory and copying elements.

4. Strings

Rust provides two primary string types: `String` and string slices (`&str`). The `String` type is a growable, heap-allocated data structure, while `&str` is a view into a string slice that can point to string literals or parts of other strings.

```rust
let mut my_string = String::from("Hello");
my_string.push_str(", world!");
```

Memory Management

The `String` type automatically handles memory deallocation when it goes out of scope, ensuring that memory leaks are avoided—a fundamental tenet in systems programming.

5. Hash Maps

The `HashMap<K, V>` data structure is used to create associative arrays, allowing for key-value pair storage. It is highly useful in situations where quick look-up times are essential. The underlying implementation employs a hashing algorithm for efficient data retrieval.

```rust
```

```rust
use std::collections::HashMap;

let mut scores = HashMap::new();
scores.insert(String::from("Blue"), 10);

scores.insert(String::from("Yellow"), 50);
```

Performance Consideration

While `HashMap` provides average O(1) time complexity for insertions and look-ups, the performance can be affected by the choice of hash function and load factors.

6. Linked Lists

Rust's standard library does not include a linked list, but developers can create one using the `Rc` and

`RefCell` types for smart pointer management. A linked list provides a flexible structure for applications requiring frequent insertions and deletions.

```rust
use std::rc::Rc;

use std::cell::RefCell;


struct Node { value: i32,

next: Option<Rc<RefCell<Node>>>,

}

let head = Rc::new(RefCell::new(Node { value: 1, next: None }));
```

Use Cases

Although linked lists are less cache-friendly compared to vectors, they are ideal for scenarios with non-contiguous memory allocation needs, such as certain algorithms that require backtracking.

7. Sets

Rust provides sets through the `HashSet` collection. They are useful when unique elements need to be stored and managed efficiently. Similar to `HashMap`, `HashSet` allows you to perform standard set operations.

```rust
use std::collections::HashSet;

let mut set: HashSet<i32> = HashSet::new(); set.insert(1);

set.insert(2);
```

Performance Consideration

`HashSet` also features average O(1) time complexity for basic operations; thus, it's suitable for scenarios demanding significant performance, such as algorithm optimizations and managing state.

In systems programming, choosing the right data structure is crucial for performance and safety. Rust provides a robust arsenal of data structures, from basic types to sophisticated collections designed for high-level functionality without sacrificing efficiency. Understanding how to leverage arrays, vectors, strings, hash maps, linked lists, and sets will enhance your ability to write performant and reliable systems software in Rust.

Chapter 3: Memory Management in Rust

In many programming languages, this challenge can lead to issues such as memory leaks, segmentation faults, and undefined behaviors. However, Rust approaches memory management with a unique philosophy that emphasizes safety and performance without a garbage collector. This chapter delves into Rust's innovative memory management model, including its ownership system, borrowing, and lifetimes.

3.1 Ownership

At the core of Rust's memory management is the concept of ownership, which ensures that each value in the program has a single owner at any given time. This principle is enforced at compile time, meaning that potential memory management issues can be caught before the code is even run.

3.1.1 The Rules of Ownership

Rust's ownership model is based on three simple rules:

Each value in Rust has a variable that's its owner.

A value can have only one owner at a time.

When the owner of a value goes out of scope, Rust will automatically drop the value, freeing the memory.

These rules prevent data races and ensure memory safety. For example, when an owner variable goes out of scope, Rust calls the `drop` function to free the associated memory, preventing memory leaks that can occur in other languages with manual memory management.

3.1.2 Moving and Copying

In Rust, ownership can be transferred using the concept of "moving". When a variable is assigned to another variable, the value is moved, and the original variable can no longer be used. This contrasts with types that implement the `Copy` trait, such as integers and booleans, where the value is copied rather than moved.

Understanding the difference between moving and copying is crucial for effective memory management in Rust applications.

```rust
fn main() {
let x = String::from("hello"); let y = x; // Move occurs here
// println!("{}", x); // This line would cause a compile-time error
}
```

By forcing developers to acknowledge ownership transfers, Rust eliminates dangling pointers and reduces the risk of unintended behavior.

3.2 Borrowing

Borrowing in Rust allows a function to use a value without taking ownership of it. This is vital for enabling shared access to data while ensuring that the safety guarantees of Rust's ownership model are maintained.

3.2.1 Mutable and Immutable Borrowing

Rust allows two types of borrowing: immutable and

mutable.

- **Immutable Borrowing**: You can borrow a value as immutable, allowing multiple parts of your code to read the data but not modify it. This is crucial for read-only access where data consistency must be maintained.

```rust
fn main() {
let s = String::from("hello");
let r1 = &s; // immutable borrow
let r2 = &s; // another immutable borrow
println!("{} and {}", r1, r2);
}
```

- **Mutable Borrowing**: A value can also be borrowed as mutable, allowing only one mutable reference to be active at a time. This prevents data races by ensuring exclusivity during modifications.

```rust
fn main() {
let mut s = String::from("hello"); let r1 = &mut s; // mutable borrow
r1.push_str(", world"); // modified through mutable reference
// println!("{}", s); // This line would cause a compile-time error
}
```

```
```

The restriction on mutable references promotes safer concurrency practices, allowing developers to write highly concurrent programs without fear of data corruption.

3.3 Lifetimes

Lifetimes in Rust provide a way to specify how long references should be valid. While ownership ensures that every piece of data has a clear owner, lifetimes help the compiler ensure that references do not outlive the data they point to, preventing dangling references.

3.3.1 Defining Lifetimes

Lifetimes are indicated using a syntax that involves apostrophes, such as `'a`. The Rust compiler uses these annotations to guarantee that references remain valid. Lifetimes can be explicit or inferred, depending on the complexity of the code.

```rust
fn longest<'a>(s1: &'a str, s2: &'a str) -> &'a str { if s1.len() > s2.len() { s1 } else { s2 }
}
```

In this example, the function `longest` takes two string slices with the same lifetime `'a` and returns a string slice that is guaranteed to be valid for that same lifetime.

3.3.2 Lifetime Elision

In many straightforward cases, Rust can infer lifetimes, and developers do not need to annotate them. For instance, if a function takes references as parameters and returns one, Rust will often automatically infer that the output reference has the same lifetime as the input references.

```rust
// Lifetime elision: Rust infers the lifetimes here fn first_word(s: &str) -> &str {
// ...
}
```

3.4 Memory Safety and Concurrency

Rust's memory management model contributes to building safe, concurrent applications. By ensuring that data can either be read or modified at any point but not both simultaneously, Rust mitigates classic concurrency issues such as data races.

In concurrent programming, Rust enforces ownership and borrowing rules across threads, providing developers with a powerful toolset to write safe and fast concurrent applications without sacrificing memory safety.

By putting these concepts at the forefront, Rust not only enhances memory safety but also empowers developers to write efficient software without the overhead of traditional garbage collection mechanisms. As we continue exploring Rust throughout the rest of this book, remember that these core principles of memory management will serve as the foundation for building robust and safe applications.

Safe and Unsafe Memory Access

This chapter will delve into the concepts of safe and unsafe memory access in Rust, exploring how Rust's ownership model contributes to safer programming while also addressing scenarios where developers may need to resort to unsafe code. We will also examine practical implications for operating system (OS) development, where low-level memory interactions are often paramount.

Understanding Memory Safety in Rust

At the heart of Rust's design is a strong emphasis on memory safety. Rust employs a unique ownership system composed of three key components: ownership, borrowing, and lifetimes. This system helps to enforce the rules around how memory is accessed and manipulated, making it impossible to have data races, null pointer dereferencing, or buffer overflows in safe Rust code.

Ownership

In Rust, each piece of memory is owned by a variable. When that variable goes out of scope, Rust automatically cleans up the memory, preventing memory leaks. This strict ownership model allows programmers to reason about memory usage without needing to explicitly manage allocation and deallocation.

Borrowing

Rust allows for borrowing of variables through references. A variable can be borrowed either mutably or immutably, but not both at the same time. This guarantees that there can only be one mutable reference or multiple immutable references, effectively preventing data races in concurrent scenarios.

Lifetimes

Lifetimes are annotations that describe the scope during which a reference is valid. They help the Rust compiler ensure that references do not outlive the data they point to, thus avoiding dangling pointers. The compiler checks lifetime annotations at compile time, which further enhances memory safety.

Safe Memory Access

Safe Rust enforces strict compile-time checks to prevent any form of unsafe access to memory. This includes performing checks on references to ensure that they do not outlive their backing data, enforcing borrowing rules, and preventing concurrent mutable access.

Examples of Safe Memory Access

Immutable References:

```rust
fn main() {
let data = 42;
let ref1 = &data; // Immutable borrow
let ref2 = &data; // Another immutable borrow
println!("Ref1: {}, Ref2: {}", ref1, ref2);
}
```

Mutable References:

```rust
```

```rust
fn update_value(value: &mut i32) {
*value += 1;
}
fn main() {
let mut data = 10; update_value(&mut data);
println!("Updated value: {}", data);
}
```

In both examples, Rust's compiler ensures that memory access adheres to safety rules, allowing developers to write reliable code without fear of memory-related bugs.

Unsafe Memory Access

Despite Rust's robust safety guarantees, there are instances—particularly in systems programming—where developers may need to perform operations that the compiler cannot verify as safe. This is where unsafe Rust comes into play.

Unsafe Code

Unsafe code blocks allow developers to perform operations that bypass some of Rust's safety guarantees. This includes raw pointer manipulation, unchecked indexing, and interfacing with foreign function interfaces (FFI). Unsafe code must be explicitly marked using the `unsafe` keyword.

Examples of Unsafe Memory Access

Raw Pointers:

```rust
```

```rust
fn unsafe_pointer_example() { let value: i32 = 42;
let ptr: *const i32 = &value;
unsafe {
println!("Value via pointer: {}", *ptr);
}
}
```

Calling External Libraries:
```rust
extern "C" {
fn external_function();
}
unsafe { external_function();
}
```

In these examples, the `unsafe` keyword signals to the compiler that the programmer is taking responsibility for the correctness and safety of the code within the block. This allows for low-level operations, but it also places the burden of safety on the developer, requiring meticulous attention to detail.

When to Use Unsafe Code

Using unsafe code should be approached cautiously:

Performance-critical sections: In an operating system, performance can be paramount. Unsafe code might be necessary when every cycle counts.

Interfacing with hardware: Directly accessing memory-mapped I/O regions often requires unsafe code.

Working with legacy systems or libraries: When integrating with existing C libraries, unsafe code enables the necessary FFI.

Implications for Operating Systems

When developing operating systems in Rust, the balance between safe and unsafe memory access is crucial. OS kernels and low-level components often require interacting with hardware and performing operations that involve the risk of undefined behavior if not managed correctly. Rust's design enables developers to write robust components while providing flexibility where low-level access is necessary.

Leveraging Safe Rust for Core Components

Many parts of an OS can be safely implemented using Rust's features. Components like file systems, process management, and memory management can utilize Rust's ownership and borrowing system to ensure safe concurrency and prevent common pitfalls.

Utilizing Unsafe Rust for Performance

However, the kernel's critical real-time performance demands may lead to sections of code that require unsafe operations. Here, careful audits and thorough testing must be applied to ensure that the use of unsafe blocks does not compromise the overall safety of the OS.

By distinguishing between safe and unsafe memory access, Rust enables developers to harness the benefits of low-level programming while minimizing the typical risks associated with such tasks. Whether leveraging safe Rust for system components or using unsafe code strategically, the dual approach supports the development of robust, efficient, and secure operating systems.

Allocators and Memory Layout in Low-Level Rust

One of the core features that enable these qualities is Rust's approach to memory management. In this chapter, we will delve into the concepts of allocators and memory layout in low-level Rust. Understanding these aspects is critical for writing efficient and safe code that interacts closely with hardware and system resources.

1. What are Allocators?

In Rust, an allocator is a component responsible for managing memory allocation and deallocation. Allocators are crucial when you need dynamic memory management, that is, allocating memory at runtime. Rust's default allocator, `malloc` from the system's standard library, provides a general-purpose memory management facility. However, Rust allows you to use custom allocators for specialized needs, such as optimizing for speed or minimizing fragmentation.

1.1 The Role of Allocators

The primary roles of an allocator include:

Allocating Memory: Reserving a specific amount of memory for use by the program.

Deallocating Memory: Reclaiming memory that is no longer in use to prevent memory leaks.

Alignment: Ensuring that memory addresses conform to certain alignment constraints, crucial in low- level programming to prevent hardware exceptions.

1.2 Using Custom Allocators

In Rust, you can define a custom allocator by implementing the `GlobalAlloc` trait. This enables you to create highly optimized memory management strategies when working on performance-critical applications. To use a custom allocator, you typically use the `#[global_allocator]` attribute. For example, consider the following code snippet:

```rust
use std::alloc::{GlobalAlloc, Layout}; struct MyAllocator;

unsafe impl GlobalAlloc for MyAllocator {

unsafe fn alloc(&self, layout: Layout) -> *mut u8 {

// Custom allocation logic here

}

unsafe fn dealloc(&self, ptr: *mut u8, layout: Layout) {

// Custom deallocation logic here

}

}

#[global_allocator]

static GLOBAL: MyAllocator = MyAllocator;
```

In this example, we define a simple structure for our allocator and implement the `alloc` and `dealloc` methods. This illustration captures the essence of a custom allocator and sets the stage for deep dive into memory management.

2. Memory Layout in Rust

Rust allows you to control memory layout, which is essential for high-performance low-level programming. Rust's memory model is built on top of a binary representation, where data structures can be carefully aligned and packed in memory for optimal size and access speed.

2.1 Data Types and Memory Representation

Rust features several primitive data types, such as integers, floating-point numbers, and compound types like structs and enums. Each type has a predetermined size and alignment, which dictates how it is stored in memory.

Size: The number of bytes occupied by a type.

Alignment: The memory address boundaries on which a type can be safely placed.

When creating data structures, you can use the `#[repr(C)]` annotation to enforce a specific order for fields, ensuring compatibility with C and other languages that rely on predictable layouts.

Example:
```rust #[repr(C)]
struct MyStruct { a: u32,

b: u64,

}
```

```
```

This code snippet guarantees that the `MyStruct` fields are laid out in the order defined, ensuring interoperability with C code.

2.2 Structs: Packing and Alignment

Rust allows you to control how fields in structs are laid out in memory. By default, Rust optimizes for alignment, which can lead to padding. However, developers can manipulate layout with `#[repr(packed)]`. This attribute can be useful in scenarios where memory is constrained:

```rust
#[repr(packed)] struct PackedStruct{

a: u8,

b: u64,

}
```

Here, `PackedStruct` sacrifices alignment guarantees to minimize memory use. However, developers must handle potential misalignment issues, especially when interacting with hardware.

3. Memory Safety and Ownership

The strength of Rust lies in its ownership model, which ensures memory safety without needing a garbage collector. Each value in Rust is owned by a variable, and memory is automatically reclaimed when it goes out of scope. This guarantees that there are no dangling pointers or use-after-free errors.

3.1 Borrowing

Rust's borrowing system allows references to data without taking ownership. This model enables safe concurrent access, as long as mutable and immutable references are used correctly. Understanding the borrowing rules is crucial when working with raw pointers or creating your own allocator, as improper usage could lead to safety violations.

3.2 Raw Pointers

In some low-level scenarios, you may need to work with raw pointers (`*const T` and `*mut T`). Rust allows the use of unsafe blocks to perform operations on raw pointers, obtaining fine-grained control over memory. However, it also places the onus of safety on the developer, who must ensure that operations do not violate Rust's safety guarantees.

```rust
let a = 10;

let ptr: *const i32 = &a; unsafe {

println!("Value at ptr: {}", *ptr);

}
```

Allocators and memory layout are foundational concepts in low-level Rust programming. Understanding how to define custom allocators and manipulate memory layout allows developers to write efficient, safe, and predictable code. As Rust continues to evolve, mastering these core principles will empower developers to leverage Rust's strengths in systems programming and performance-critical applications. In the following chapters, we will explore how to apply these concepts in real-world scenarios and best practices for implementing robust and efficient Rust solutions.

Chapter 4: Concurrency and Parallelism in Rust

They enable developers to write software that can handle multiple tasks simultaneously, enhancing responsiveness and throughput. Rust, designed with performance and safety in mind, offers robust abstractions for concurrency and parallelism, making it a prime candidate for building scalable applications.

Concurrency refers to the ability of a program to manage multiple tasks that may be running simultaneously but do not necessarily execute at the same time. It allows for interleaved execution, where the context switches between tasks, giving the illusion of simultaneous execution. This is especially useful in I/O-bound applications where waiting for resources can be done while other tasks are processed.

Parallelism, on the other hand, involves the simultaneous execution of multiple tasks. It capitalizes on multi-core processors where separate threads can perform computations at the same time, improving performance for computation-heavy applications.

This chapter will explore how Rust facilitates concurrency and parallelism through its ownership model, threading capabilities, and libraries, as well as best practices for implementing these concepts in Rust applications.

4.1 The Rust Ownership Model

Rust's unique ownership model is instrumental in providing safe concurrency. At its core, the model ensures memory safety without a garbage collector, which is essential when dealing with multiple threads. The key elements of Rust's ownership model include:

Ownership: Each value in Rust has a single owner, which is responsible for cleaning up that value when it goes out of scope.

Borrowing: Rust allows for references to a value without taking ownership, enabling multiple parts of a program to read from the same data.

Mutability: Mutability in Rust is controlled, allowing either one mutable reference or multiple immutable references at a time, preventing data races.

These principles create a strong foundation for building concurrent applications, as they eliminate common pitfalls such as data races and deadlocks.

4.1.1 Data Races and Safety

A data race occurs when multiple threads access the same mutable data simultaneously, which can lead to unpredictable results. Rust's ownership and borrowing rules inherently prevent data races. By restricting how data can be shared and modified across threads, Rust ensures that programs are thread-safe by design.

For instance, consider the following code snippet that attempts to share mutable state across threads:

```rust
use std::thread;
fn main() {
let mut number = 5;
let handle = thread::spawn(move || {
```

```
number += 1; // This will cause a compile-time error.
});
handle.join().unwrap();

}
```
` ` `

In the above example, Rust will not compile the code because `number` is being moved into the thread and then modified. Since Rust prevents mutable references from being shared, the developer must resort to a safe way of sharing data.

4.2 Threading in Rust

Rust provides a powerful standard library for threading, making it easy to work with multiple threads. The key features of Rust's threading model include:

Threads: Rust allows the creation of threads using the `std::thread` module. Each thread can run concurrently and can be spawned using `thread::spawn`.

Data Sharing: There are multiple ways to safely share data between threads, including:

Mutex: A mutual exclusion primitive that protects shared data. Only one thread can access the data at a time.

RwLock: A reader-writer lock that allows multiple readers or one writer.

Arc: An atomic reference counter that enables shared ownership of values across threads. ### 4.2.1 Using Mutex

Here is an example of how to use a `Mutex` to safely

share data between threads:

```rust
use std::sync::{Arc, Mutex}; use std::thread;

fn main() {

let counter = Arc::new(Mutex::new(0)); let mut handles = vec![];

for _ in 0..10 {

let counter = Arc::clone(&counter); let handle = thread::spawn(move || {

let mut num = counter.lock().unwrap();

*num += 1;

});

handles.push(handle);

}

for handle in handles { handle.join().unwrap();

}

println!("Result: {}", *counter.lock().unwrap());

}
```

In this example, we created a shared `counter` protected by a `Mutex`, allowing multiple threads to safely increment its value.

4.3 Asynchronous Programming

Rust also supports asynchronous programming, which is particularly beneficial for I/O-bound tasks. The `async` and `await` keywords allow you to write code that performs operations concurrently without blocking threads. Rust's async model is built on futures, representing values computed asynchronously.

4.3.1 Using `async` and `await`

Here's a simple example of asynchronous programming in Rust:

```rust
use tokio;

#[tokio::main] async fn main() {
let future1 = async { 1 }; let future2 = async { 2 };

let result = future1.await + future2.await; println!("Result: {}", result);
}
```

In this snippet, two futures are created and run concurrently, with the results combined afterward. Tokio, a popular asynchronous runtime for Rust, provides tools for managing asynchronous tasks efficiently.

4.4 Parallelism in Rust

When it comes to parallelism, Rust offers robust libraries such as `rayon`, which makes data parallelism simple and easy to implement. Rayon enables you to perform operations on collections in parallel without detailed thread management.

4.4.1 Using Rayon for Parallel Processing

Here's an example of using Rayon to compute the sum of a large range of numbers in parallel:

```rust
use rayon::prelude::*;

fn main() {

let sum: u64 = (1..=1_000_000).into_par_iter().sum();
println!("Sum: {}", sum);

}
```

In this code, `into_par_iter` converts the range into a parallel iterator, and `sum` computes the total in parallel, leveraging available cores effectively.

4.5 Best Practices

While Rust's features make it easier to write safe concurrent and parallel code, here are some best practices to keep in mind:

Embrace Ownership and Borrowing: Understanding and using Rust's ownership model will help prevent common concurrency issues.

Limit Shared State: Where possible, minimize shared mutable state. Prefer message-passing paradigms, such as channels, to communicate between threads.

Use Tools: Leverage existing libraries like Rayon and Tokio to simplify parallelism and asynchronous programming.

Profile and Benchmark: Always measure performance improvements and ensure that concurrency or parallelism

59

adds value to your application.

By leveraging its ownership model, threading capabilities, and asynchronous programming features, developers can create efficient, robust applications capable of handling concurrent tasks and parallel computations with ease. Understanding and properly implementing concurrency and parallelism will not only enhance application performance but will also significantly improve the reliability of your Rust programs.

Managing Threads Safely with Rust

Managing threads safely can be a challenging task, especially in languages that do not emphasize safety and concurrency guarantees. Rust, with its emphasis on memory safety and data race prevention, provides a compelling solution to these challenges. This chapter will explore Rust's threading model, its concurrency primitives, and best practices for managing threads safely.

Understanding Threads in Rust

In Rust, a thread is a sequence of instructions that can be run independently from another sequence. Threads allow a program to do multiple tasks simultaneously, but improper handling can lead to problems like data races, deadlocks, and resource contention.

Creating Threads

Rust provides the `std::thread` module for working with threads. The most basic way to create a thread is by using the `thread::spawn` function, which takes a closure as an argument:

```rust
use std::thread;
fn main() {
let handle = thread::spawn(|| { for i in 1..5 {
println!("Hello from the thread! {}", i);
}
});
for i in 1..5 {
println!("Hello from the main thread! {}", i);
}
// Wait for the thread to finish handle.join().unwrap();
}
```

In this example, a new thread is spawned that prints messages, while the main thread does the same. We ensure that the main thread waits for the child thread to complete using `handle.join()`.

Ownership and Concurrency

A significant aspect of Rust's safety guarantees is its ownership model, which helps prevent common concurrency issues like data races. In Rust, data can either be owned by one thread at a time or shared across threads using synchronization primitives.

Moving Ownership

When you spawn a thread, you have the option to move ownership of variables into the closure. This is important because if you allow multiple threads to own a variable, it can lead to data races. Here's how to move ownership:

```rust
use std::thread;

fn main() {

let value = String::from("Hello, World!"); let handle = thread::spawn(move || {

println!("{}", value);

});

// Wait for the thread to finish handle.join().unwrap();

}
```

In this example, the `move` keyword ensures that the `value` is moved into the thread, providing exclusive ownership. This prevents concurrent access from the main thread, making it safe.

Sharing Data

Sometimes, we need to share data between threads. Rust provides several mechanisms for this, the most common being `Arc` (Atomic Reference Counted) and `Mutex` (Mutual Exclusion).

Using Arc

`Arc` allows safe sharing of data across threads. It is a thread-safe version of `Rc`, enabling multiple ownership without the risk of invalidation.

```rust
```

```rust
use std::sync::{Arc, Mutex}; use std::thread;
fn main() {
let counter = Arc::new(Mutex::new(0)); let mut handles =
vec![];
for _ in 0..10 {
let counter = Arc::clone(&counter); let handle =
thread::spawn(move || {
let mut num = counter.lock().unwrap();
*num += 1;
});
handles.push(handle);
}
for handle in handles { handle.join().unwrap();
}
println!("Result: {}", *counter.lock().unwrap());
}
```
```

In this example, multiple threads increment a shared counter safely using `Mutex`. The `Arc` ensures that the counter remains valid as long as it is needed by any thread.

#### Deadlocks and Avoiding Them

While using `Mutex` is effective, it can lead to deadlocks if not handled correctly. A deadlock occurs when two or more threads wait on each other to release locks. To minimize the risk of deadlocks:
```

Lock Order: Always acquire locks in a consistent order.

Scope Locks: Keep the scope of locked data as short as possible.

Avoid Nested Locks: If possible, avoid locking more than one resource at a time. ## Thread Pools

Creating and managing threads individually can incur significant overhead. Instead, Rust's ecosystem provides thread pool implementations, such as `rayon` and `std::thread::spawn`. These libraries handle the management of threads for you, allowing you to focus on your task.

Using Rayon for Parallelism

Rayon is a popular crate for data parallelism in Rust. You can easily parallelize operations on collections with minimal effort:

```rust
use rayon::prelude::*;

fn main() {

let nums = vec![1, 2, 3, 4, 5];

let squares: Vec<_> = nums.par_iter().map(|&x| x * x).collect(); println!("{:?}", squares);

}
```

In this example, `rayon` allows you to apply a mapping function to each element of a vector in parallel.

Rust provides powerful tools and guarantees for managing

threads safely. By leveraging its ownership model, and concurrency primitives like `Arc` and `Mutex`, developers can write concurrent code without the usual pitfalls of data races and deadlocks. Additionally, libraries like Rayon enable easy parallelization, making it simpler to harness the power of concurrent execution. As you continue to explore concurrency in Rust, adhere to best practices to ensure safe and efficient thread management in your applications.

Building Efficient Concurrent Systems

In this chapter, we'll explore how Rust, with its unique ownership model and emphasis on safety, provides a robust foundation for building efficient concurrent systems. We'll delve into the principles of concurrency, the tools and patterns available in Rust, and best practices for developing concurrent applications.

1. Understanding Concurrency

Concurrency refers to the ability of a system to manage multiple tasks at the same time. In a concurrent system, tasks can be executed in overlapping time periods, which is particularly useful for I/O-bound operations, parallel computations, and responsive UIs.

In the context of Rust, concurrency is not just about performing tasks simultaneously; it's about doing so safely. The Rust programming language emphasizes memory safety and prevents data races at compile time. This unique characteristic is vital for creating reliable concurrent systems.

1.1 Data Races and Safety

A data race occurs when two or more threads access the same memory location concurrently, and at least one of the accesses is a write. Data races can lead to unpredictable behavior and subtle bugs that are often hard to debug. Rust's ownership system, which includes the concepts of borrowing and lifetimes, is designed to eliminate data races:

Ownership: Each piece of data in Rust has a single owner. When the owner goes out of scope, the data is automatically deallocated.

Borrowing: Data can be borrowed in two ways: mutably or immutably. Only one mutable reference is allowed at a time, while multiple immutable references can coexist. This system ensures that data is accessed safely across threads.

2. The Tooling of Concurrency in Rust

Rust provides several powerful abstractions and libraries for achieving concurrency. The main tools include: ### 2.1 Threads

Rust's standard library provides a thread module that allows the creation and management of threads. The

`std::thread` module supports spawning threads, where each thread runs concurrently with others. Here's a simple example:

```rust
use std::thread;
fn main() {
let handle = thread::spawn(|| { for i in 1..5 {
```

```rust
        println!("Thread: {}", i);
    }
});
for i in 1..5 { println!("Main: {}", i);
}
handle.join().unwrap();
}
```

In this example, a new thread is spawned to execute a block of code, running concurrently with the main thread.

2.2 Channels

Channels facilitate communication between threads. Rust provides a multi-producer, single-consumer (mpsc) channel that allows messages to be sent from one thread to another, facilitating safe data sharing across threads.

```rust
use std::sync::mpsc; use std::thread;
fn main() {
let (tx, rx) = mpsc::channel();
thread::spawn(move || {
let msg = String::from("Hello from the thread!");
tx.send(msg).unwrap();
});
let received = rx.recv().unwrap(); println!("Received: {}",
received);
```

```
}
```
```

In this example, the main thread sends a message to another thread through a channel, showcasing how threads can communicate safely.

### 2.3 Async/Await

Rust's asynchronous programming model, introduced in Rust 1.39, provides another avenue for building concurrent systems through the use of async functions and the await mechanism. Using the `async-std` or `tokio` libraries, Rust enables writing asynchronous code that can handle high levels of concurrency without blocking.

Here's a simple example of an asynchronous function:

```rust
use async_std::task;

async fn say_hello() { println!("Hello, async world!");
}
fn main() { task::block_on(say_hello());
}

```

In this code, the `say_hello` function is defined as asynchronous, allowing it to be awaited when executed. Asynchronous programming is particularly useful for I/O-bound applications, such as web servers and networked
```

services.

3. Patterns for Concurrency ### 3.1 The Actor Model

The Actor Model is a popular concurrency model that can be effectively implemented in Rust. Actors are independent entities that encapsulate state and communicate through message passing. This model fits well with Rust's emphasis on safety.

Using libraries such as `actix`, developers can build applications where each actor corresponds to a specific behavior, interacting with other actors by sending messages.

3.2 Fork/Join Parallelism

Rust's capabilities allow you to implement fork/join parallelism using threads. Developers can spawn a number of threads to perform computations and then join the results. This pattern is particularly useful for CPU-bound tasks, like image processing or numerical calculations.

Here's an example illustrating the fork/join concept:

```rust
use std::thread;

fn main() {

let handles: Vec<_> = (0..10).map(|i| {
thread::spawn(move || {

println!("Thread number: {}", i);

})

}).collect();
```

```
for handle in handles { handle.join().unwrap();
}
}
```
` ` `

In this example, multiple threads are spawned, each performing a concurrent operation. ## 4. Best Practices for Writing Concurrent Code in Rust

Use Safe Abstractions: Rely on channels, mutexes, and other synchronization primitives provided by the standard library or community libraries to manage shared state safely.

Minimize Shared State: Aim for a design that reduces the need for shared mutable state, which can lead to complexity and potential data races.

Profile and Optimize: Use Rust's built-in tools and libraries for profiling concurrent applications, identifying bottlenecks, and optimizing performance.

Test Thoroughly: Concurrent code can be challenging to test. Use unit tests, integration tests, and consider tools like `cargo fuzz` for testing concurrent applications against race conditions.

By leveraging threads, channels, and async programming, Rust enables developers to write robust, high-performance applications that fully utilize the capabilities of modern hardware. As we continue to strive for greater efficiency in software, understanding and mastering concurrency in Rust will be essential for creating tomorrow's applications.

Chapter 5: Building a Minimal Operating System Kernel

Operating systems are the backbone of computing, managing hardware resources and providing essential services for applications. In recent years, Rust has emerged as a powerful programming language for systems programming, known for its performance and memory safety. This chapter will guide readers through the process of building a minimal operating system kernel in Rust, covering key concepts, tools, and code examples.

5.1 Introduction to Operating Systems

Before diving into kernel development, it's crucial to have a foundational understanding of operating system concepts. An operating system (OS) serves as an intermediary between computer hardware and applications. Its primary functions include:

Resource management: Allocating CPU, memory, and I/O resources to various tasks.

Process management: Creating, scheduling, and terminating processes.

Memory management: Tracking memory usage, allocating and freeing memory as needed.

Device management: Facilitating communication between the OS and peripheral devices.

A kernel is the core component of an operating system, responsible for managing system resources and enabling communication between hardware and software. Our focus will be on developing a minimal kernel that provides basic functionality, which can serve as a foundation for

71

more complex features.

5.2 Setting Up the Development Environment

To start building a kernel in Rust, we need to set up a suitable development environment. Below are the essential tools and steps for getting started:

5.2.1 Install Rust

Install the Rust toolchain by following these commands:

```bash
curl --proto '=https' --tlsv1.2 -sSf https://sh.rustup.rs | sh
source $HOME/.cargo/env
```

5.2.2 Install Additional Tools

You'll need `rustup` and `cargo`, along with some target options for building a kernel. These can be installed using:

```bash
rustup target add x86_64-unknown-none
```

5.2.3 Configure Cargo

To successfully build the kernel, you'll need to set up a new project. Create a new directory for your kernel and navigate into it:

```bash
cargo new rust_os --bin cd rust_os
```

Then, modify the `Cargo.toml` to include the necessary

dependencies:

```toml
[package]
name = "rust_os" version = "0.1.0"
edition = "2021"
[profile.dev] panic = "abort"
[profile.release] panic = "abort"
[dependencies]
volatile = "0.6.0"   # For direct memory access
x86_64 = "0.14.0"   # For expertise in x86_64 architecture
```

5.3 Writing a Simple Kernel ### 5.3.1 The Main Function

The entry point of our kernel will be a function called `_start`. Within this function, we will set up basic features and enter an infinite loop. Begin by creating a new Rust file named `main.rs` under `src`:

```rust
#![no_std] // No standard library #![no_main] // No main entry point
// Panic handler
use core::panic::PanicInfo;
#[panic_handler]
fn panic(_info: &PanicInfo) -> ! { loop {}
}
```

```rust
// Kernel entry point #[no_mangle]
pub extern "C" fn _start() -> ! {
// Initialization logic here (e.g., setting up the screen) loop
{}
}
```

5.3.2 Setting Up the Screen

In a real kernel, you would need to communicate with hardware, such as the display. Below is an example of how to set up a simple text-mode interface on a VGA screen.

Create a new module for VGA text buffer:

```rust
mod vga_buffer { use core::fmt;

pub struct Writer;

impl fmt::Write for Writer {

fn write_str(&mut self, s: &str) -> fmt::Result {
// Code to write to the VGA buffer Ok(())
}
}

pub fn print(s: &str) {
// Access the VGA buffer and print strings
}
}
```

5.3.3 Coupling the Kernel and VGA

Modify the `_start` function to use the VGA module, printing "Hello, World!" to the screen:

```rust
#[no_mangle]

pub extern "C" fn _start() -> ! { vga_buffer::print("Hello, World!"); loop {}

}
```

5.4 Compiling the Kernel

Now that our kernel code is ready, we need to compile it for our target architecture. Use the following commands to create an executable:

```bash

cargo build --target x86_64-unknown-none.json
```

5.4.1 Creating a Custom Target Specification

Create a custom target specification file named `x86_64-unknown-none.json`:

```json

{

"arch": "x86_64",

"os": "none",

"vendor": "unknown",

"linker": "x86_64-unknown-none-gnu", "llvm-target": "x86_64-unknown-none", "enable-cxx-abi": false,
```

```
"no-compiler-rt": true, "panic-abort": true, "test": false,
"pre-link-args": { "gcc": [
"-Tlinker.ld",
]
}
}
```
` ` `

5.5 Finding and Fixing Errors

Kernel development often involves debugging low-level issues. When running the kernel, be prepared to handle potential errors related to memory access, hardware issues, and mismatches in the compilation target.

5.5.1 Common Debugging Strategies

Use a serial port for logging information.

Implement simple logging directly to the console.

Utilize QEMU or another emulator to test your kernel without real hardware.

In this chapter, we introduced the process of building a minimal operating system kernel in Rust. We set up our development environment, wrote a simple kernel that can print text to the screen, and learned how to compile and run our kernel in an emulator. Building a kernel is a complex and rewarding task that lays the foundation for further exploration into operating systems, Rust programming, and system-level programming.

Bootstrapping the Kernel with Rust

Historically, kernel development has predominantly relied on languages like C due to its performance characteristics and low-level access to hardware. However, C's lack of inherent safety features has led to countless vulnerabilities and bugs. With the rise of Rust, a systems programming language designed with safety and concurrency in mind, there is a growing interest in using Rust to develop kernels. This chapter explores the principles, methodologies, and practical steps involved in bootstrapping a kernel using Rust.

---

1. Understanding the Concept of Bootstrapping

Bootstrapping, in a computing context, refers to the process of starting up a system from a basic state. It typically involves loading a minimal piece of software that initializes the hardware and loads the operating system kernel. In the context of Rust, bootstrapping has unique challenges due to language features, safety guarantees, and the necessity for a corresponding runtime.

1.1 Bootstrapping in C vs. Rust

Traditionally, in C, the bootstrap process relies on a simple assembly routine that sets up the stack and jumps into the C runtime. In contrast, Rust introduces a higher level of abstraction and enforcement of safety, which requires a different approach to the bootstrap process. Rust aims to eliminate data races and null pointer dereferencing, thus changing how we think about kernel initialization.

---

2. Why Rust for Kernel Development? ### 2.1 Safety Guarantees

Rust's borrowing and ownership system helps prevent data races and memory leaks, making it an attractive choice for critical system components like a kernel. Its compile-time checks ensure that many errors that would typically lead to system crashes are caught early.

2.2 Performance

Rust offers zero-cost abstractions and fine-grained control over memory layout without sacrificing performance. This allows kernel developers to write code that is not only safe but also highly efficient.

2.3 Concurrency

Rust's rich type system and concurrency model allow for safe parallelism, reducing the risk associated with multi-threaded kernel operations.

---

3. Setting Up the Environment

To begin bootstrapping a kernel with Rust, setting up the development environment is essential. This includes the installation of Rust, target specifications, and necessary tools.

3.1 Prerequisites

Rust Toolchain: Install the latest stable version of Rust. Using `rustup` is highly recommended as it simplifies managing Rust versions and toolchain components.

Target Specification: Create a target specification for the architecture on which you intend to run your kernel. This includes settings for memory layout, panic handlers, etc.

Build Tools: Tools like `bootimage` and `cargo-xbuild` are necessary for creating bootable images. ### 3.2 Creating a New Rust Project

With Rust installed, we can start a new project for the kernel:

```bash
cargo new rust_kernel --bin cd rust_kernel
```

Edit the `Cargo.toml` to set the appropriate dependencies:

```toml
[package]
```

name = "rust_kernel" version = "0.1.0"

[dependencies]

dependencies specific to kernel development (no_std, alloc, etc.)
```
```

---

4. Writing the Kernel Code

The next phase involves writing the actual kernel code. The kernel code is composed primarily of Rust with some inline assembly for low-level operations.

4.1 The Entry Point

Define the entry point using a "no-std" environment since you won't have access to standard libraries:

```rust
```rust #![no_std] #![no_main]

use core::panic::PanicInfo; #[no_mangle]

pub extern "C" fn _start() -> ! {

// Initialization code goes here loop {}
}

#[panic_handler]

fn panic(_info: &PanicInfo) -> ! { loop {} }
}
```
```

4.2 Memory Management

Managing memory in a kernel is complex, and Rust's features can help. Implementing a simple memory allocator and integrating it into the kernel environment is crucial for dev.

4.3 Interrupt Handling

Creating a mechanism for handling interrupts in Rust effectively requires defining a structure for interrupts and implementing safe concurrent data structures as needed.

---

5. Compiling and Testing

Once the basic structure of the kernel is in place, it must be compiled to a binary format that can be booted. We will set up `cargo` to produce a bootable image:

```bash
cargo build --target your_target_spec.json
```

Using `bootimage`, we can create a disk image to test in a virtual machine:

```bash
cargo bootimage --target your_target_spec.json
```

5.1 Testing in a Virtual Machine

Using tools like QEMU, we can simulate the booting process:

```bash
qemu-system-x86_64                          -drive
format=raw,file=target/your_target/debug/bootimage-
rust_kernel.bin
```

---

6. Future Prospects and Considerations

The use of Rust in kernel development is still in the early stages, but it is gaining traction in various projects. Continued contributions from the community and improvements in tooling will pave the way for broader adoption. Considerations such as interface stability, community guidelines, and collaboration with existing projects will be paramount in enhancing the ecosystem.

Bootstrapping a kernel with Rust merges the efficacy of low-level programming with safety and modern concurrency paradigms. The transition from traditional languages like C introduces a wealth of possibilities while mitigating common pitfalls. As developers continue to explore and refine this approach, the future of operating system development looks promising and efficient, ultimately leading to more reliable and maintainable solutions.

Basic Kernel Architecture and Execution Flow

Rust offers memory safety, concurrency, and performance without the overhead of garbage collection, making it an ideal candidate for kernel programming. In this chapter, we will explore the basic architecture of a kernel written in Rust and the execution flow of programmatic operations within it.

1. Understanding Kernel Architecture ### 1.1 What is a Kernel?

At its core, a kernel is the central part of an operating system that manages system resources and allows hardware and software to communicate. It acts as a bridge between applications and the underlying hardware, ensuring that processes run efficiently and securely.

1.2 Key Components of Kernel Architecture

A typical kernel consists of several components, each of which plays a crucial role in the overall operation. In the context of Rust, these components emphasize safety and concurrency.

Process Management: Responsible for managing process creation, scheduling, and termination. Rust's type system helps in preventing data races in concurrent executions.

Memory Management: Manages memory allocation and deallocation, ensuring that programs do not overwrite each other's memory. Rust's ownership model significantly reduces memory-related bugs seen in traditional C/C++ kernels.

Device Drivers: Interfaces that allow the kernel to communicate with hardware devices. Rust's abstractions can provide better safety guarantees compared to traditional approaches.

File Systems: Manages data storage and retrieval. Rust's type system and pattern matching capabilities allow for more robust file system implementations.

Inter-process Communication (IPC): Allows processes to communicate with one another safely and efficiently. Rust's message-passing concurrency model can facilitate reliable IPC mechanisms.

1.3 Microkernel vs. Monolithic Kernel

Rust can be employed in both microkernel and monolithic kernel architectures.

Monolithic Kernel: All services run in kernel space, which can lead to performance advantages but greater complexity and risk.

Microkernel: Only the most essential services run in kernel space, with others running in user space for added safety. Rust's modularity allows for an easier implementation of microkernel concepts.

2. Execution Flow in Kernel

Understanding execution flow is critical for developing efficient and safe kernel code. Let's break it down into stages:

2.1 Booting the System

When a system powers on, the bootloader initializes the hardware and loads the kernel into memory. In Rust, this initial stage involves creating a binary that sets up the basic environment for the kernel to operate.

Example Rust code for setting up a basic kernel:

```rust
#![no_std] #![no_main]
use core::panic::PanicInfo; #[no_mangle]
pub extern "C" fn _start() -> ! {
// Initialization code goes here. loop {}
}
#[panic_handler]
fn panic(_info: &PanicInfo) -> ! { loop {}
}
```

2.2 Kernel Initialization

Once loaded, the kernel performs a series of initialization tasks:

Setting up memory management structures.

Initializing process scheduling systems.

Loading device drivers.

In Rust, initialization functions can be structured using async and await, which allow for non-blocking operations. This facilitates a more responsive and efficient boot process.

2.3 Running User Processes

After initialization, the kernel begins executing user processes. The execution flow involves:

Process Creation: A request for a new process triggers the creation of a virtual address space for it.

Context Switching: The kernel uses a scheduler to switch between processes, leveraging Rust's

`std::thread` and other concurrency primitives.

Executing System Calls: User applications interact with the kernel through system calls. The kernel translates these calls into direct hardware interactions.

2.4 Interrupt Handling

Interrupts are signals from hardware that require immediate attention from the kernel. The Rust kernel handles these through interrupt descriptors, allowing for efficient servicing of hardware events.

Example snippet of an interrupt handler in Rust:

```rust
use riscv::register::mie;

#[no_mangle]
```

```
pub extern "C" fn interrupt_handler() {
// Handle the interrupt
// Clear the interrupt
}
fn enable_interrupts() { unsafe {
mie::set_mie();
}
}
```
` ` `

2.5 Cleanup and Termination

When a process completes its execution or is terminated, the kernel must restore the system to a stable state. This involves deallocating memory, notifying other processes, and removing the process from the scheduling queue. Rust's ownership model ensures that resources are released safely, preventing memory leaks.

The concepts explored in this chapter—such as process and memory management, interrupt handling, and the role of the Rust type system—highlight the potential of Rust in systems programming. As operating systems evolve, and the demand for secure, concurrent applications grows, Rust stands as a formidable candidate for the future of kernel development. With strong community support and ongoing research, the potential of building robust kernels using Rust is only beginning to be realized.

Chapter 6: Interfacing with Hardware

This chapter delves into the principles and techniques needed to interact effectively with hardware components. Whether to control motors, read sensor data, or facilitate communication between devices, understanding hardware interfacing is foundational for building robust and exciting projects.

6.1 Understanding Hardware Interfaces ### 6.1.1 Types of Hardware Interfaces

There are several types of hardware interfaces that engineers commonly encounter. Understanding these will help you choose the right system for your project.

Digital Interfaces: These use binary signals (0s and 1s) to communicate. Examples include GPIO (General Purpose Input/Output), I^2C (Inter-Integrated Circuit), SPI (Serial Peripheral Interface), and UART (Universal Asynchronous Receiver-Transmitter).

Analog Interfaces: These transmit data in continuous waveforms. Examples include voltage levels for sensors, where varying voltage corresponds to different measured values (such as temperature or light intensity).

Bluetooth and Wi-Fi: These are wireless interfaces used for connecting devices without physical links, allowing data transmission over protocols like TCP/IP.

6.1.2 Protocols and Standards

Protocols ensure that devices can communicate effectively and consistently. Familiarize yourself with common protocols used in interfacing, including:

I^2C: A multi-master, multi-slave, packet-switched, single-ended communication bus.

SPI: High-speed synchronous data transfer, often used for memory chips and displays.

UART: A hardware communication protocol that uses asynchronous serial communication. ### 6.1.3 Hardware Abstraction Layers (HAL)

Many programming environments and frameworks offer Hardware Abstraction Layers (HAL) to simplify the process of interfacing with hardware. HAL provides a consistent interface to access and control hardware devices, allowing developers to write code without needing to worry about the underlying complexity of the hardware.

6.2 Selecting the Right Components

6.2.1 Choosing Microcontrollers and Processors

Microcontrollers (MCUs) and processors are the brains behind embedded systems. Factors to consider when selecting an MCU include:

Processing Power: Clock speed, architecture, and core count.

I/O Options: Number and type of I/O ports required for interfacing with sensors and actuators.

Power Consumption: Especially crucial for battery-operated devices.

Examples of popular MCUs include the Arduino platform (specifically the AVR series), Raspberry Pi, and more specialized options like STM32 or ESP32, which offer integrated Wi-Fi capabilities.

6.2.2 Sensors and Actuators

Choosing the right sensors and actuators is critical to the success of your project. Sensors convert physical phenomena into electronic signals, while actuators perform actions based on received signals. Key considerations include:

Sensor Type: Choosing between digital or analog based on the requirements of your application.

Range and Sensitivity: Ensure the sensor can measure the phenomenon accurately within your required range.

Compatibility: Confirm that the sensor or actuator is compatible with your chosen microcontroller. ## 6.3 Practical Interfacing Techniques

6.3.1 Connecting Components

Understanding how to physically connect components is crucial. Diagrams and schematics can help visualize connections. Common methods include:

Breadboarding: A prototyping tool that allows for easy insertion and removal of components.

Wiring: Use jumper wires to connect components on a breadboard or PCB (Printed Circuit Board). Pay attention to the pin configuration to avoid short circuits.

6.3.2 Reading Sensor Values

Once hardware is connected, reading sensor values systematically is essential. This involves:

Initialization: Setting up the microcontroller to

recognize and communicate with the sensor correctly.

Data Acquisition: Using the appropriate protocols to acquire data. For example, with I^2C sensors, you may use specific libraries available in environments like Arduino IDE to read values seamlessly.

6.3.3 Controlling Actuators

Controlling actuators is often just as important as reading sensors. Techniques include:

Analog Output: Using PWM (Pulse Width Modulation) to control the speed of motors or brightness of LEDs.

Digital Signals: Sending high or low signals to toggle relays or switches that control larger devices. ### 6.3.4 Debugging and Troubleshooting

No interfacing project is complete without a debugging phase. Tools like multimeters, oscilloscopes, and logic analyzers can be invaluable for troubleshooting issues. Common problems may include:

Incorrect Connections: Double-check wiring and connections to ensure everything is as planned.

Incorrect Programming: Ensure the code you've written matches the hardware setup, taking care of timing and protocol settings.

6.4 Case Study: Building a Simple Weather Station

To solidify the concepts covered in this chapter, let's consider a case study where we build a simple weather station that measures temperature and humidity.

6.4.1 Components Required

Microcontroller: Arduino Uno

Sensors: DHT11 (Temperature and Humidity sensor)

Display: LCD module to show readings

Power Supply: USB or battery pack ### 6.4.2 Wiring Setup

Using a breadboard, wire the DHT11 sensor and the LCD display to the Arduino Uno following the specific pinout for each component.

6.4.3 Code Implementation

Using the Arduino IDE, write the code that initializes the sensors, reads data, and displays it. Libraries for both the DHT11 and the LCD module will streamline the programming process.

6.4.4 Testing

Upload the code to the Arduino, power the project, and watch the data display live on the LCD. Use an external tool to measure the actual temperature and humidity to validate your readings.

This chapter has provided you with a structured approach to understanding hardware interfaces, selecting components, implementing practical interfacing techniques, and even building a prototype project. As you encounter real-world applications, the skills learned here will serve as the foundation for tackling increasingly complex systems as you venture into the exciting world of embedded systems and hardware interfacing.

Writig Device Drivers in Rust

Device drivers are crucial components of an operating system that allow higher-level application software to communicate with hardware devices. They act as translators between the hardware and the applications that use them, enabling the OS to control the hardware without needing to understand its intricacies. Traditional device driver development has often been associated with low-level programming languages like C, primarily due to their performance and direct access to hardware resources.

However, with the rise of Rust, developers have begun exploring its potential in this domain. Rust's strong emphasis on memory safety, concurrency, and performance makes it an attractive choice for writing device drivers. This chapter will dive deep into the fundamentals of device driver development using Rust, covering its advantages, basic structures, and the practicalities of building drivers.

Why Rust for Device Drivers? ### Memory Safety

One of the primary advantages of Rust is its focus on memory safety. Rust's ownership system prevents common bugs such as null pointer dereferencing and buffer overflows, which are prevalent in C/C++ driver development. By catching these issues at compile time rather than runtime, Rust helps developers create more robust and secure drivers.

Concurrency

Rust's approach to concurrency, with its borrowing system, allows developers to write concurrent code safely and effectively. This is particularly important in driver development, where operations may be performed simultaneously across multiple threads or processes.

Performance

Rust is designed to be a systems programming language, offering performance that is comparable to C and C++. This performance is critical for device drivers that often operate at the boundary of hardware capability.

Community and Ecosystem

The Rust community is rapidly growing, and the ecosystem is becoming increasingly rich with libraries and frameworks that simplify the development process. Projects like `rusty-driver` provide tools and abstractions that help facilitate driver development.

Understanding the Basics of Device Drivers ### Types of Device Drivers

Character Drivers: These are used for devices that perform sequential I/O operations (e.g., keyboards, mice).

Block Drivers: Used for devices that read/write data in blocks (e.g., hard drives).

Network Drivers: Specifically designed for network interface cards (NICs), allowing communication over a network.

Architecture of Device Drivers

A typical device driver consists of several key components:

Initialization and Cleanup: Code that sets up the driver and releases resources when the driver is no longer needed.

File Operations: Functions that handle file-like operations (open, read, write, close).

Interrupt Handling: Mechanisms to respond to hardware interrupts.

IOCTL (Input/Output Control): Custom commands to communicate specific actions to the driver. ### Writing Your First Device Driver in Rust

Here's an overview of how you might start to write a simple character device driver in Rust. #### Setting Up the Environment

Before writing the driver, ensure you have the Rust toolchain and necessary dependencies installed. You will need to set up a cargo project and include relevant crates for kernel development.

```bash
cargo new rust_char_driver cd rust_char_driver
```

Make sure to update the `Cargo.toml` file to include dependencies necessary for kernel development. You might want to use `rust_kernel` or other similar crates available in the ecosystem.

Basic Structure of a Character Driver

A basic skeleton for a character device driver might look like this:

```rust
#![no_std] // Use no_std for kernel programming
#![feature(impl_trait_in_bindings)]
```

```rust
use kernel::prelude::*; use kernel::chrdev;
module! {
name: b"rust_char_driver", authors: &[b"Your Name"],
description: b"A simple Rust character device driver.",
license: b"GPL",
}
// Structure representing the driver state struct
RustCharDriver {
_chardev: Option<chrdev::Registration>,
}
// Implement the driver logic
impl KernelModule for RustCharDriver { fn init() ->
Result<Self> {
pr_info!("Rust Char Driver Initialized\n");
let                    _chardev              =
chrdev::Registration::new::<RustCharDriver>(
cstr!("rust_char"), // Device name

0, // Major number (0 means use dynamic)
)?;
Ok(RustCharDriver {
_chardev: Some(_chardev),
})
}
}
```

```rust
// Define file operations
impl FileOpener for RustCharDriver {
fn open(ctx: &FileOpenContext) -> Result<Self> {
pr_info!("Device opened by PID: {}\n", ctx.task().pid());
Ok(RustCharDriver { _chardev: None }) // Return driver instance
}
}
// ...
// Register and unregister driver impl Drop for RustCharDriver {
fn drop(&mut self) {
pr_info!("Rust Char Driver Unloaded\n");
}
}
```

Compilation and Testing

Once you have your code ready, compile it using Rust's cargo tool, and ensure you have a kernel build environment set up. Load the driver into your Linux kernel using `insmod`, and interact with it using standard file operations.

Handling Errors and Debugging

Driver development can be tricky due to the low-level nature of the code. Rust's error handling model provides a clean way to manage errors. Use the `Result` type to handle potential failures gracefully.

Additionally, debugging drivers typically involves using kernel messages (`pr_info!`, `pr_err!` etc.) to trace operations.

Best Practices in Device Driver Development

Modular Design: Keep your driver modular and well-documented to ease maintenance and updates.

Error Handling: Implement robust error handling to prevent crashes and undefined behavior.

Testing: Thoroughly test drivers in a controlled environment before deployment, as kernel-level bugs can result in system instability.

Leverage Rust's Ecosystem: Utilize existing crates and community resources to simplify your development process.

Writing device drivers in Rust represents a promising direction for systems programming, balancing performance with safety. While it requires a conceptual leap for those accustomed to C/C++, Rust's advantages in memory safety and concurrency make it an excellent choice for modern driver development.

Working with Memory-Mapped I/O

In Rust, working with MMIO can be both efficient and safe, taking advantage of Rust's ownership model and its guarantees about data races. This chapter aims to guide you through the principles of MMIO in Rust, including setup, accessing memory-mapped registers, and ensuring safe concurrent access.

Understanding Memory-Mapped I/O

In traditional I/O operations, the CPU communicates with hardware devices using special instructions. In contrast, MMIO maps hardware device registers directly into the system's address space. This means that instead of issuing specific input/output commands, programs read from and write to specific addresses in memory that correspond to various device functions.

Benefits of Memory-Mapped I/O

Simplicity: Once the device is mapped into memory, standard data manipulation techniques can be used.

Speed: In many cases, MMIO can lead to performance improvements by avoiding context switches between user mode and kernel mode.

Flexibility: MMIO can be used with various types of devices—from graphics cards to network adapters—allowing for a consistent programming model across hardware.

Setting Up for MMIO in Rust ### Requirements

Before diving into the code, make sure you have the following:

Rust installed on your system.

A compatible hardware device that uses MMIO.

The `volatile` crate added to your `Cargo.toml` for safely accessing memory-mapped registers.

```toml [dependencies] volatile = "0.2"
```

```
```

Accessing the MMIO Region

To map a hardware device's registers, you'll typically need to know the base address of its MMIO region. This base address is often provided by the hardware documentation or can be obtained from the operating system during initialization.

```rust
const DEVICE_BASE: usize = 0x4000_0000; // Example base address for a hypothetical device const DEVICE_SIZE: usize = 0x1000; // Size of the MMIO region

fn initialize_device() {

// Safety: Mapping the base address to a mutable slice of a certain size let device_memory = unsafe {

core::slice::from_raw_parts_mut(DEVICE_BASE      as *mut u32, DEVICE_SIZE / 4)

};

// Initialize the device, e.g., writing configuration values device_memory[0] = 0x01; // Writing to a register

}
```

The `unsafe` block is necessary because directly manipulating raw pointers can lead to undefined behavior if not employed with caution.

Reading and Writing MMIO Registers

Using the `volatile` crate, you can perform read and write

operations on memory-mapped registers without the compiler optimizing them away.

```rust
use volatile::Volatile;
struct Device {
register: Volatile<u32>,
}
impl Device {
fn new(base_addr: usize) -> Self { Device {
register: Volatile::new(base_addr as *mut u32),
}
}
fn read_register(&self) -> u32 { self.register.read()
}
fn write_register(&self, value: u32) {
self.register.write(value);
}
}
fn main() {
// Create a device at the specified base address let device =
Device::new(DEVICE_BASE);
// Write a value to a register
device.write_register(0x1234_5678);
// Read the value back
```

```
let value = device.read_register(); println!("Read value:
{:X}", value);

}
```

In this example, a `Device` struct wraps a memory-mapped device register, utilizing the `Volatile` type from the `volatile` crate. This abstraction helps prevent any unintended optimization, ensuring that reads and writes are actually performed.

Safety and Concurrency ### Safe Access Patterns

Even though Rust provides powerful safety guarantees, MMIO often involves hardware that can behave unpredictably, particularly with concurrent access from multiple threads or interrupts. Here are some strategies to ensure safety:

Mutexes: When sharing access between threads, consider using `std::sync::Mutex` to lock access to the device.

Atomic Operations: Where appropriate, utilize `std::sync::atomic` types to perform atomic reads and writes to shared registers.

Memory Barriers: MMIO may necessitate memory barriers to ensure that operations are performed in a specific order.

Example Using Mutex

```rust
use std::sync::{Arc, Mutex}; use std::thread;

let                       device                      =
```

101

```
Arc::new(Mutex::new(Device::new(DEVICE_BASE))); let
handles: Vec<_> = (0..10).map(|i| {

let device_clone = Arc::clone(&device);

thread::spawn(move || {

let    mut    dev    =    device_clone.lock().unwrap();
dev.write_register(i);

println!("Thread {} wrote value {}", i, i);

})

}).collect();

for handle in handles { handle.join().unwrap();

}
```
```

In the above example, we allow multiple threads to safely write to the same MMIO device by wrapping the

`Device` instance in an `Arc<Mutex<_>>`.

The Rust programming language provides robust tools for working with memory-mapped I/O, leveraging its strong safety features while allowing for low-level hardware interaction. By following the principles outlined in this chapter—including proper setup, utilizing volatile memory access patterns, and understanding concurrency—developers can efficiently and safely work with hardware devices.
```

Chapter 7: Interrupt Handling in Rust

As operating systems evolve to handle more complex hardware and software interactions, the need for safe and effective interrupt handling becomes paramount. In this chapter, we delve into the principles of interrupt handling and how Rust, with its emphasis on safety and concurrency, provides unique advantages in this critical area of OS development.

7.1 Understanding Interrupts ### 7.1.1 What is an Interrupt?

An interrupt is a signal sent to the processor that temporarily halts the current execution context, allowing the system to address an event that requires immediate attention. Interrupts can be generated by hardware (like input/output devices) or software (such as system calls). When an interrupt occurs, the processor saves its current state, switches to a special routine known as an interrupt handler, processes the interrupt, and then resumes its previous task.

7.1.2 Types of Interrupts

Hardware Interrupts: Generated by peripherals, such as keyboards or network cards, to flag that they need processing.

Software Interrupts: Triggered by programs when they need to request services from the OS, often leading to context switches.

Timer Interrupts: Regularly triggered interrupts allowing the OS to manage time and schedule tasks.

Understanding these types and their purposes is crucial

for developing an efficient interrupt handling mechanism.

7.2 The Role of the Operating System

The operating system plays a key role in managing interrupts. It is responsible for:

Prioritizing Interrupts: Some interrupts must be handled more urgently than others.

Context Switching: The OS must save the state of the current task and load the state of the interrupt handler efficiently.

Handling Race Conditions: Concurrency introduces the risk of race conditions, particularly when interrupts can occur while accessing shared resources.

7.3 Interrupt Handling in Rust

7.3.1 Why Rust for Interrupt Handling?

Rust's design philosophy emphasizes memory safety, concurrency, and performance. This makes it an excellent fit for low-level systems programming, including interrupt handling. Key features include:

Ownership and Borrowing: Rust's ownership model ensures that memory safety is guaranteed at compile time, preventing common errors like null pointer dereferences and buffer overflows.

Concurrency without Data Races: Rust's type system allows developers to write concurrent code without the risk of data races, which is especially important during interrupt servicing.

7.3.2 Setting Up an Interrupt Handler

Setting up an interrupt handler in Rust involves several

components:

Define the Interrupt Vector: The interrupt vector table contains addresses of all interrupt handlers. Rust allows low-level manipulation through `unsafe` code when interfacing with hardware.

```rust
#[no_mangle]
pub extern "C" fn interrupt_handler() {
// Your interrupt handling logic here
}
```

Registering Interrupt Handlers: The OS must register handlers for specific interrupts.

```rust
fn register_interrupt_handler(interrupt_number: u8, handler: fn()) {
// Implementation to link handler with interrupt number
}
```

Handling Context Switching: When an interrupt occurs, the OS must save the current context and switch to the interrupt context, involving careful stack management.

7.3.3 Safety and Concurrency Considerations

When dealing with interrupts, the following Rust features can be used to maintain safety in shared state:

- **Atomic Types**: `std::sync::atomic` provides atomic

operations for safely sharing data across threads and handlers.

```rust
use std::sync::atomic::{AtomicUsize, Ordering};

static INTERRUPT_COUNTER: AtomicUsize = AtomicUsize::new(0); fn interrupt_handler() {

INTERRUPT_COUNTER.fetch_add(1, Ordering::SeqCst);

}
```

- **Mutexes and Locks**: Use `std::sync::Mutex` with caution since hold-lock could lead to deadlocks if not carefully managed during an interrupt.

7.4 Implementing an Example Interrupt Handler

In this section, we implement a simple interrupt handler in Rust that counts the number of interrupts received from a hypothetical hardware device.

7.4.1 Setting Up the Environment

Start by configuring a new Rust project with the appropriate dependencies for OS development. Typically, this might involve using the `no_std` environment.

7.4.2 Writing a Simple Interrupt Handler

Here is an example of an interrupt handler that increments a counter every time it is called:

```rust #![no_std] #![no_main]
```

```rust
use core::panic::PanicInfo;

use core::sync::atomic::{AtomicUsize, Ordering};

static INTERRUPT_COUNT: AtomicUsize = AtomicUsize::new(0); #[no_mangle]

pub extern "C" fn interrupt_handler() {

// Increment the interrupt count atomically
INTERRUPT_COUNT.fetch_add(1, Ordering::SeqCst);

// Further processing can be done here
}

#[panic_handler]

fn panic(_info: &PanicInfo) -> ! { loop {} }

}
```

7.4.3 Testing Your Handler

To test the interrupt handler, simulate interrupts in a controlled environment. This involves writing test harnesses that can trigger the handler repeatedly, verifying that the count increments as expected.

In this chapter, we explored the intricacies of interrupt handling in the context of operating systems and highlighted how Rust provides powerful abstractions for safe and efficient interrupt management. By leveraging Rust's ownership model, type system, and concurrency features, developers can create robust and safe interrupt handlers.

Understanding Interrupts and Exception Handling

Rust, a language renowned for its emphasis on safety and performance, provides unique abstractions that make interrupt and exception handling more manageable while ensuring that common pitfalls like race conditions and memory safety issues are mitigated. This chapter delves into understanding these concepts within the context of Rust programming.

1. Background on Interrupts and Exceptions

Before we dive into Rust's handling of these concepts, it's essential to understand what interrupts and exceptions are.

1.1 Interrupts

Interrupts are signals that divert the CPU's attention from the current execution flow to handle a different task or event. They can be triggered by hardware (like I/O operations) or software (through system calls). The interrupt handling process generally involves:

Context Switch: Saving the current state of the CPU and loading the state of the interrupt handler.

Execution of the Handler: Running specific code to handle the interrupt.

Restoration: Restoring the previous state after the interrupt code has executed. ### 1.2 Exceptions

Exceptions are conditions that disrupt the normal flow of execution in a program, typically due to errors, like accessing invalid memory, arithmetic errors, or overflows. In Rust, exceptions typically manifest through `panic!` conditions, which can occur for various reasons such as assertion failures or attempts to unwrap an

`Option` that is `None`.

2. Handling Interrupts in Rust

Rust is generally employed for systems programming due to its ability to write low-level code safely. When handling interrupts, direct access to hardware might be necessary. The Rust ecosystem has several crates (libraries) that can aid in writing interrupt handlers for embedded systems or operating systems.

2.1 Crate Examples

`embedded-hal`: This crate provides traits that represent hardware abstractions. When writing interrupt handlers for microcontrollers, you might implement these traits to handle various hardware events.

`rtic`: Real-Time Interrupt-driven Concurrency (RTIC) is an ecosystem aimed at providing efficient and safe concurrency in embedded systems. It offers a way to define concurrent tasks, handle interrupts, and manage shared resources without the usual risks associated with concurrency.

2.2 Writing an Interrupt Handler

Here is a simplified example of how you might define and register an interrupt handler in Rust:

```rust #![no_std] #![no_main]

use cortex_m::interrupt::free; use cortex_m_rt::entry;

use panic_halt as _;
```

```
#[entry]
fn main() -> ! {
// Initialization code...
loop {
// Main loop...
}
}
#[interrupt]
fn EXAMPLE_INTERRUPT() {
// Handle the interrupt... free(|cs| {
// Access shared resources safely
});
}
```
```

In this example, we use the `#[interrupt]` attribute to denote an interrupt handler in an embedded environment. The `free` function is used to gain mutable access to shared resources safely.

### 2.3 Safety and Concurrency

When writing interrupt handlers, it is vital to ensure that access to shared data is thread-safe. Rust's ownership model helps mitigate common issues such as data races, making it a powerful tool in systems programming.

## 3. Exception Handling in Rust

Rust's approach to error handling is nuanced. Instead of
```

using traditional exception handling mechanisms, Rust employs the type system to enforce error handling at compile time, primarily through `Result<T, E>` and `Option<T>` types.

3.1 The Panic Paradigm

In Rust, a `panic!` is a mechanism that indicates a serious error that the program cannot recover from. When a panic occurs, Rust unwinds the stack, cleaning up resources until it reaches a point where it can safely terminate. The following code snippet illustrates a panic scenario:

```rust
fn main() {
let number: Option<i32> = None;


// This will trigger a panic because we are trying to unwrap a None value let value = number.unwrap();
}
```

3.2 Recovering from Panics

While direct recovery from panics is often discouraged (as it could lead to inconsistent program states), Rust offers the `std::panic::catch_unwind` function, which allows you to catch panics and handle them gracefully if desired.

```rust
use std::panic;
fn main() {
```

```rust
let result = panic::catch_unwind(|| { let number:
Option<i32> = None;

// This will trigger a panic number.unwrap();
});


match result {

Ok(_) => println!("No panic occurred!"), Err(_) =>
println!("A panic occurred!"),
}
}
```

3.3 Error Handling Best Practices

Rust encourages explicit error handling. Instead of
panicking, you should strive to handle possible errors
gracefully using the `Result` type. For example:

```rust
fn perform_operation() -> Result<i32, String> {

// Some operation that may fail

if true { // replace with actual conditions Ok(42)
} else {

Err("Operation failed".to_string())
}
}
fn main() {
```

```
match perform_operation() {

Ok(value) => println!("Operation succeeded with value: {}", value), Err(e) => println!("Error encountered: {}", e),

}

}
```
` ` `

Understanding interrupts and exception handling is fundamental for developing reliable Rust applications, especially in systems programming contexts. Rust's unique approach—leveraging its ownership model, type system, and concurrency paradigms—provides a safer environment for managing the complexities of interrupts and exceptions. By adhering to the principles outlined in this chapter, developers can write code that is not only efficient but also resilient against many common programming errors.

Implementing an Interrupt Descriptor Table (IDT)

In this chapter, we will delve into the implementation of an IDT in Rust, a systems programming language that offers memory safety without sacrificing performance. We will go through the fundamental concepts, define the necessary data structures, and implement basic operations needed to setup an IDT.

Understanding the Interrupt Descriptor Table (IDT)

Before we jump into the Rust implementation, it's essential to understand what an IDT is and its role in the

Interrupt Handling Mechanism:

What is an IDT?

The IDT is a data structure used by the CPU to define how to handle interrupts. Each entry in the IDT corresponds to a specific interrupt vector and contains the address of the interrupt handler as well as other attributes such as privilege levels.

Interrupt Vectors

Interrupts are numbered from 0 to 255, with each number corresponding to a specific type of interrupt (hardware or software). The IDT allows the system to vector these interrupts to the appropriate handlers.

Handler Functions

When an interrupt occurs, the system saves the current execution state and jumps to the interrupt handler defined in the IDT, allowing the program to manage the interrupt before returning to its previous workflow.

Setting Up the Rust Environment

Before we begin coding, ensure that you have the Rust toolchain installed. If you are working within a bare-metal environment, you will also require a suitable toolchain that supports no_std operations.

```bash
rustup target add x86_64-unknown-none
```

This target is appropriate for writing system-level code without the standard library. ## Step 1: Defining IDT Entry

First, let's define the basic structure of an IDT entry in Rust. Each entry typically consists of a handler function address, selector, type attributes, and flags.

IDT Entry Definition

```rust
#[repr(C)]  struct IdtEntry {
offset_low: u16, selector: u16, ist: u16, type_attr: u8,
offset_middle: u16, offset_high: u32,
reserved: u32,
}
```

Explanation

`offset_low`, `offset_middle`, `offset_high`: These fields hold the address of the interrupt handler.

`selector`: This field selects the segment descriptor for the interrupt.

`ist`: Interrupt Stack Table index (for stack switching).

`type_attr`: This field defines the type and attributes of the descriptor (e.g., if it is present, privilege level).

`reserved`: A reserved field for future use or alignment.

Step 2: Writing the IDT

Next, we will define the IDT itself, which will be an array of `IdtEntry` structs. We will also implement a function to initialize the IDT.

```rust
const IDT_SIZE: usize = 256;
struct Idt {
```

```rust
    entries: [IdtEntry; IDT_SIZE],
}
impl Idt {
pub fn new() -> Self { Idt {
    entries: [IdtEntry { offset_low: 0,
    selector: 0,
    ist: 0,
    type_attr: 0,
    offset_middle: 0,
    offset_high: 0,
    reserved: 0,
    }; IDT_SIZE],
}
}
pub fn set_entry(&mut self, vector: usize, handler: usize,
selector: u16, type_attr: u8) { let low = handler as u32 &
0xFFFF;
let middle = (handler as u32 >> 16) & 0xFFFF; let high =
(handler >> 32) as u32;
self.entries[vector] = IdtEntry { offset_low: low as u16,
selector,
ist: 0, type_attr,
offset_middle: middle as u16, offset_high: high,
reserved: 0,
```

```
};
    }
}
```

Notes on the Implementation

The `Idt` struct holds an array of `IdtEntry` elements.

The `set_entry` method allows us to populate an entry in the IDT using the interrupt vector, the handler address, selector, and type attributes.

Step 3: Loading the IDT

After we have defined our IDT, we need to load it into the CPU's IDT register. This requires using inline assembly. The x86 architecture provides the `lidt` instruction for this purpose.

Loading IDT in Rust

```rust
#[inline(always)]
unsafe fn load_idt(idt: &Idt) {
    let idt_ptr = idt.entries.as_ptr() as u64;
    let idt_descriptor = ((idt.entries.len() * core::mem::size_of::<IdtEntry>()) as u16) << 16) | (idt_ptr as u16);

    asm!("lidt [{}]", in(reg) &idt_descriptor);
}
```

Explanation

We build the IDT descriptor that combines the size of the IDT and the pointer to the IDT itself using a bitwise OR operation.

The `lidt` instruction is invoked using inline assembly to load our IDT. ## Step 4: Setting Up Interrupt Handlers

With the IDT set up, it's time to create and link custom handlers to our IDT: ### Example Interrupt Handler

```rust
extern "C" fn my_interrupt_handler() {
// Handle the interrupt (for demonstration)
// This is where you add your interrupt-specific logic
}
```

Registering the Handler

```rust
fn main() {
let mut idt = Idt::new();


// Registering interrupt handlers
idt.set_entry(0, my_interrupt_handler as usize, 0x08, 0x8E); // example handler setup for vector 0 unsafe {
load_idt(&idt);
}
//    Enable    interrupts    (implementation-specific)
```

```
enable_interrupts();
}
```
```
```

We covered defining the IDT structure, setting entries, loading the IDT into the CPU, and creating custom interrupt handlers.

By understanding and implementing the IDT, you have taken significant strides in low-level programming with Rust, opening doors to more complex systems programming tasks such as operating system development and hardware programming.

Chapter 8: Filesystems and Storage Management

This chapter delves into the workings of filesystems and storage management in Rust, illustrating how to handle files, directories, and various storage media, while maintaining Rust's safety guarantees.

8.1 Understanding Filesystems

A filesystem is the method by which data is stored and organized on storage devices. Different operating systems implement various filesystems, such as NTFS, ext4, and FAT32. In Rust, interactions with these filesystems are abstracted through the standard library and external crates that provide higher-level functionalities.

8.1.1 Key Concepts of Filesystems

Files and Directories: At the core of any filesystem are files and directories. Files store data, while directories organize files into a hierarchical structure.

Paths: A filesystem path specifies the location of a file or directory. Rust provides representations of filesystem paths through the `Path` and `PathBuf` types in the `std::path` module.

Metadata: Filesystems also maintain metadata about files and directories, such as creation time, modification time, size, and permissions.

8.2 The Rust Standard Library for Filesystem Operations

Rust's standard library includes functionalities for handling file I/O which are essential for filesystem management. The `std::fs` module provides several methods for the creation, reading, writing, and deletion of files and directories.

8.2.1 Basic File Operations #### Creating a File

To create and write to a file, you can use the `File::create` function:

```rust
use std::fs::File; use std::io::Write;

fn create_file() -> std::io::Result<()> {

let mut file = File::create("example.txt")?;
file.write_all(b"Hello, Rust!")?;

Ok(())

}
```

Reading from a File

You can read a file's contents using the `read_to_string` method:

```rust
use std::fs::File;

use std::io::{self, Read};
```

```rust
fn read_file() -> io::Result<String> {
```

let mut file = File::open("example.txt")?; let mut contents = String::new(); file.read_to_string(&mut contents)?; Ok(contents)

```
}
```
```

### 8.2.2 Directory Operations

Working with directories involves creating, removing, and iterating over directory entries:

```rust
use std::fs; use std::io;
```

fn list_dir() -> io::Result<()> { for entry in fs::read_dir(".")? {

let entry = entry?;

println!("{}", entry.file_name().into_string().unwrap());

} Ok(())

```
}
```
```

8.2.3 Metadata and Permissions

Rust also allows you to access metadata about files and directories using methods like `metadata()`:

```rust
use std::fs; use std::io;
```

fn file_metadata() -> io::Result<()> {

let metadata = fs::metadata("example.txt")?; println!("File

Size: {}", metadata.len()); println!("Is Directory: {}", metadata.is_dir()); Ok(())

}
```

## 8.3 Error Handling in File I/O

Rust's approach to error handling through the `Result` type makes it easier to manage filesystem errors gracefully. Each operation that may fail returns a `Result` that you can handle appropriately using `match` statements or the `?` operator for propagation.

### 8.3.1 Example Error Handling

Consider a scenario where you attempt to read a file that may not exist. You can handle the potential error like so:

```rust
fn read_possible_file() {

match read_file() {

Ok(contents) => println!("File Contents: {}", contents),
Err(e) => eprintln!("Error reading file: {}", e),

}

}
```

8.4 Advanced Storage Management in Rust

While the standard library provides robust support for basic file operations, complex storage management might require additional libraries. Crates like `tokio` and `sled` offer asynchronous file I/O and embedded database
```

functionalities respectively.

8.4.1 Asynchronous File I/O

Using the `tokio` crate, you can perform non-blocking file operations, which is crucial for applications that demand high concurrency:

```rust
use tokio::fs;

#[tokio::main] async fn main() {

let contents = fs::read_to_string("example.txt").await.unwrap();
println!("{}", contents);

}
```

8.4.2 Embedded Databases

For applications requiring persistent data storage, the `sled` crate provides a simple embedded database that supports key-value storage without the overhead of a separate database server:

```rust
use sled;

fn main() {

let db = sled::open("my_db").unwrap(); db.insert("key", "value").unwrap();


if let Some(value) = db.get("key").unwrap() {

println!("Found key: {}", String::from_utf8(value.to_vec()).unwrap());
```

124

```
}
}
```
` ` `

The utilization of the standard library, coupled with external crates, empowers developers to build efficient systems capable of handling complex requirements in file I/O and data storage. As you continue your journey in Rust, keep exploring the capabilities this powerful language offers in managing data effectively and safely.

Creating a Custom Filesystem with Rust

One of the OS's most vital components is the filesystem, responsible for the storage, retrieval, and organization of data on physical devices. In this chapter, we will explore how to create a custom filesystem using Rust, a systems programming language known for its safety and performance characteristics. This guide will walk you through the fundamental concepts, design considerations, and practical implementation of a basic filesystem.

1. Understanding Filesystem Basics

Before diving into actual coding, it's essential to grasp the underlying concepts of filesystems: ### 1.1 Components of a Filesystem

A typical filesystem comprises several key components:

Inode: A data structure that stores file metadata, such as permissions, timestamps, and location on disk.

Superblock: This contains information about the filesystem as a whole, including its size, type, and the number of inodes.

Data Blocks: These are the actual storage units that hold file content.

Directories: Special files that map filenames to inode numbers, facilitating file lookup.

1.2 Filesystem Types

Different filesystem types (e.g., FAT32, NTFS, ext4) have unique designs and functionalities. For our purpose, we will create a simple custom filesystem that prioritizes learning over performance.

2. Setting Up the Rust Environment

To create a custom filesystem in Rust, you first need to set up your development environment. ### 2.1 Installing Rust

Follow these steps to install Rust:

Install Rust via rustup:

```bash
curl --proto '=https' --tlsv1.2 -sSf https://sh.rustup.rs | sh
```

Set up your development path:

```bash
source $HOME/.cargo/env
```

2.2 Create a New Rust Project Start a new project for your filesystem:

```bash
cargo new my_custom_fs cd my_custom_fs
```

```
```

3. Designing the Filesystem

In this section, we will outline the design of our custom filesystem, focusing on simplicity. ### 3.1 Defining the Structure

We will create simple structures for the inode, superblock, and directory. In `src/lib.rs`, define these structs:

```rust
#[derive(Debug)] struct Superblock {

total_blocks: u32, free_blocks: u32, inode_count: u32,

}

#[derive(Debug)] struct Inode {

file_size: u32, block_pointers: Vec<u32>,

}

#[derive(Debug)] struct Directory {

entries: Vec<(String, u32)>, // filename and inode number

}
```

3.2 Initializing the Filesystem

We need functions to initialize the superblock and the filesystem in memory.

```rust
impl Superblock {

fn new(total_blocks: u32) -> Self { Superblock {

total_blocks,
```

```
free_blocks: total_blocks, inode_count: 0,
}
}
}
```

3.3 Basic Operations

We will implement basic operations such as creating files and writing data.

```rust
impl Inode {
fn new() -> Self{ Inode {
file_size: 0,
block_pointers: Vec::new(),
}
}
}
impl Directory {
fn new() -> Self {
Directory { entries: Vec::new() }
}
fn add_file(&mut self, name: String, inode_number: u32)
{ self.entries.push((name, inode_number));
}
}
```

```
```

4. Implementing the Filesystem

With the design in place, it's time to implement the filesystem. ### 4.1 Creating Files

Create a function to read a file from memory and update the inode and directory:

```rust
fn create_file(directory: &mut Directory, name: &str, size: u32) -> Result<(), &str> { if directory.entries.iter().any(|(n, _)| n == name) {

return Err("File already exists.");

}


let inode_number = 1; // For simplicity, let's assume we use a static inode number. let mut new_inode = Inode::new();

new_inode.file_size = size;

directory.add_file(name.to_string(), inode_number);
Ok(())

}
```

4.2 Writing Data

Next, implement a function to write data into a file.

```rust
fn write_file(inode: &mut Inode, data: &[u8]) {
inode.block_pointers.push(data.len() as u32); // Store
```
129

dummy block size. inode.file_size += data.len() as u32;

```
}
```

4.3 Reading Files

Implement reading functionality based on the inode structure.

```rust
fn read_file(inode: &Inode) -> Vec<u8> {

let data_vec = vec![0u8; inode.file_size as usize]; // Dummy read data.

data_vec

}
```

5. Testing the Filesystem

Testing is critical for our filesystem's correctness. ### 5.1 Writing Tests

Add tests in `src/lib.rs` to validate our filesystem functions:

```rust
#[cfg(test)] mod tests {

use super::*;

#[test]

fn test_create_file() {

let mut directory = Directory::new();
assert_eq!(create_file(&mut directory, "test.txt", 100), Ok(())); assert_eq!(directory.entries.len(), 1);
```

```
}
#[test]
fn test_write_file() {
let mut inode = Inode::new(); write_file(&mut inode, &[1,
2, 3, 4]);
assert_eq!(inode.file_size, 4);
}
}
```
```

In this chapter, we took a high-level overview of building a
simple custom filesystem using Rust. We explored
fundamentals such as data structures used in filesystems,
established a clear design plan, and implemented core
functionalities, including creating, writing, and reading
files. While our example is simplistic, it serves as a
foundational exercise revealing how filesystem principles
can be fostered using Rust.

# Implementing Storage Drivers

With Rust's focus on safety and concurrency, it provides a
compelling programming model for implementing storage
drivers. This chapter will explore the essentials of writing
storage drivers in Rust, covering the fundamental
concepts, design principles, and practical
implementations.

## Why Rust for Storage Drivers?
```

Rust combines low-level control with high-level abstractions, making it ideal for systems programming. Its unique features, such as:

Memory Safety: Rust's ownership model ensures that memory safety issues, such as null pointer dereferencing and buffer overflows, are caught at compile time.

Concurrency: The language's design prevents data races at compile time, which is crucial for high-performance storage applications that often require concurrency.

Performance: Rust offers performance that is close to that of C and C++, enabling the development of fast and efficient storage solutions.

These features make Rust particularly suitable for writing storage drivers, which require both performance and safety to manage hardware resources correctly.

Understanding the Storage Driver Architecture

Prior to diving into coding, it's essential to understand the architecture of storage drivers. A typical storage driver interacts with both the operating system and the underlying hardware. The primary responsibilities of a storage driver include:

Device Communication: Managing communication with storage devices (like SSDs, HDDs) through appropriate protocols (e.g., SATA, NVMe).

Data Management: Handling data read/write operations, buffering, caching, and scheduling.

Error Handling: Implementing robust error handling

mechanisms to deal with hardware and communication failures.

Integration with Filesystem: Collaborating with the operating system's filesystem layer to provide a seamless data access experience.

Understanding these roles will guide you in implementing a storage driver that meets performance and reliability goals.

Setting Up Your Rust Environment

Before implementing the driver, you need to set up a Rust development environment. Follow these steps:

Install Rust: If you haven't already, install Rust using `rustup`, the Rust toolchain installer. Run the command:

```bash
curl --proto '=https' --tlsv1.2 -sSf https://sh.rustup.rs | sh
```

Set Up Your Project: Create a new Rust project using Cargo, Rust's package manager:

```bash
cargo new rust_storage_driver cd rust_storage_driver
```

Configure Dependencies: Add necessary dependencies in `Cargo.toml`. For storage drivers, consider using libraries like `tokio` for asynchronous programming and `num` for numerical operations when needed.

```toml
[dependencies]
```

```
tokio = { version = "1", features = ["full"] } num = "0.4"
```
```

## Building a Simple Block Device Driver

Let's implement a simple, illustrative block device driver.
This example will not be production-ready but will serve
to explain the underlying principles.

### Defining Block Device Structures

In Rust, you can define the structures representing your
block device. A block device typically manages fixed-size
blocks of data. Let's create the foundational structures.

```rust
#[derive(Debug)] struct BlockDevice {

blocks: Vec<u8>, // This would ideally be replaced by an
actual buffer scheme block_size: usize,

}
impl BlockDevice {

fn new(num_blocks: usize, block_size: usize) -> Self {
BlockDevice {

blocks: vec![0; num_blocks * block_size], block_size,

}
}

pub fn read_block(&self, block_index: usize) -> &[u8] {
let start = block_index * self.block_size;
&self.blocks[start..start + self.block_size]

}

pub fn write_block(&mut self, block_index: usize, data:
&[u8]) { let start = block_index * self.block_size;
```

134
```

```rust
        self.blocks[start..start                      +
self.block_size].copy_from_slice(data);
    }
}
```

Implementing I/O Operations

Next, we will implement functionality to handle reading and writing data to the block device.

```rust
#[tokio::main] async fn main() {

let block_size = 512; // 512 bytes per block

let num_blocks = 1000; // Total of 1000 blocks

let mut device = BlockDevice::new(num_blocks, block_size);

// Write data to block 0

let data_to_write = vec![1; block_size]; // Fill with 1s
device.write_block(0, &data_to_write);

// Read data back from block 0

let read_data = device.read_block(0);
assert_eq!(read_data, &data_to_write[..]);

println!("Data read from block 0: {:?}", read_data);

}
```

This code shows how to read from and write to a simple block device. The `tokio::main` function allows us to run asynchronous operations, which would be essential in a real-world scenario where I/O operations can block.

135

Error Handling

Effective error handling is a must for any storage driver. You can utilize Rust's `Result` type to manage errors gracefully.

```rust
#[derive(Debug)]
pub enum BlockDeviceError { OutOfBounds,
WriteError,
}
impl BlockDevice {
pub fn read_block(&self, block_index: usize) -> Result<&[u8], BlockDeviceError> { if block_index >= self.blocks.len() / self.block_size {
Err(BlockDeviceError::OutOfBounds)
} else {
let start = block_index * self.block_size;
Ok(&self.blocks[start..start + self.block_size])
}
}
pub fn write_block(&mut self, block_index: usize, data: &[u8]) -> Result<(), BlockDeviceError> { if block_index >= self.blocks.len() / self.block_size {
return Err(BlockDeviceError::OutOfBounds);
}
if data.len() != self.block_size {
return Err(BlockDeviceError::WriteError);
```

```
        }

        let start = block_index * self.block_size;
        self.blocks[start..start                                    +
        self.block_size].copy_from_slice(data); Ok(())
    }
}
```
```

Implementing storage drivers in Rust requires an understanding of both the hardware and the abstractions provided by the language. By leveraging Rust's features, you can create storage solutions that are not only efficient but also safe from common programming errors. This chapter has laid the groundwork for building a simple block device driver, setting the stage for more complex developments.
```

Chapter 9: Networking in Low-Level Rust

While high-level languages simplify network programming with extensive libraries and frameworks, low- level programming in Rust provides unique opportunities and challenges, especially when it comes to networking. This chapter will guide you through the process of implementing networking capabilities in Rust, focusing on the practical applications and underlying principles behind network programming in a systems language.

9.1 Understanding Networking Basics

Before diving into Rust-specific networking, it's essential to grasp the fundamentals of how computer networking operates. Network programming deals with the communication between computers over a network. The two primary protocols are:

Transmission Control Protocol (TCP): A connection-oriented protocol that ensures reliable data transmission.

User Datagram Protocol (UDP): A connectionless protocol that emphasizes speed over reliability, making it suitable for applications like video streaming or online gaming.

Understanding these protocols is crucial as they inform how data is transmitted and managed in Rust. ## 9.2 Setting Up Your Rust Environment

To implement networking in Rust, you need to ensure that you have a suitable development environment. Follow these steps to set up:

Install Rust: Use [rustup](https://rustup.rs/) to install the Rust compiler and Cargo, the Rust package manager.

```sh
curl --proto '=https' --tlsv1.2 -sSf https://sh.rustup.rs | sh
```

Create a New Project:

```sh
cargo new rust_networking cd rust_networking
```

Add Dependencies:

Although Rust's standard library provides basic networking features, there are libraries like `tokio` and `async-std` for asynchronous programming that can simplify networking. You can add dependencies in your `Cargo.toml` file.

```toml
[dependencies]
tokio = { version = "1", features = ["full"] }
```

9.3 Basic TCP Networking

To create a simple TCP server and client in Rust, you can take advantage of the `std::net` module. Here's a basic example:

9.3.1 TCP Server

First, let's create a TCP server that listens for incoming connections:

```rust
use std::net::{TcpListener, TcpStream}; use std::io::{Read, Write};

use std::thread;

fn handle_client(mut stream: TcpStream) { let mut buffer = [0; 1024];

while let Ok(size) = stream.read(&mut buffer) { if size == 0 { break; } stream.write(&buffer[0..size]).unwrap();

}

}

fn main() {

let                    listener                    = TcpListener::bind("127.0.0.1:7878").unwrap(); println!("Server listening on port 7878");

for stream in listener.incoming() { match stream {

Ok(stream) => { thread::spawn(move || {

handle_client(stream);

});

}

Err(e) => {

eprintln!("Failed to accept connection: {:?}", e);

}
```

```
}
}
}
```
` ` `

This server listens on `127.0.0.1:7878`, receives data from clients, and echoes it back. ### 9.3.2 TCP Client

Now, let's build a simple TCP client to connect to our server:

` ` `rust

use std::net::TcpStream;

use std::io::{self, Write, Read};

fn main() -> io::Result<()> {

let mut stream = TcpStream::connect("127.0.0.1:7878")?; let msg = b"Hello, server!";

stream.write(msg)?;

let mut buffer = [0; 1024];

let size = stream.read(&mut buffer)?;

println!("Received: {}", String::from_utf8_lossy(&buffer[0..size]));

Ok(())

}

` ` `

This client connects to the server, sends a message, and receives an echo response. ## 9.4 Working with UDP

UDP is useful for applications where performance is critical, and occasional packet loss is acceptable. Below is an example of a simple UDP client and server.

9.4.1 UDP Server

```rust
use std::net::{UdpSocket};

fn main() {

let socket = UdpSocket::bind("127.0.0.1:34254").expect("Could not bind socket"); let mut buf = [0; 1024];

loop {

let (amt, src) = socket.recv_from(&mut buf).expect("Failed to receive data"); println!("Received: {}", String::from_utf8_lossy(&buf[0..amt])); socket.send_to(&buf[0..amt], &src).expect("Failed to send data");

}

}
```

This server listens for incoming messages and echoes them back to the sender. ### 9.4.2 UDP Client

```rust
use std::net::{UdpSocket};

fn main() {

let socket = UdpSocket::bind("127.0.0.1:0").expect("Could not bind socket"); let msg = b"Hello, UDP server!";
```

```rust
socket.send_to(msg, "127.0.0.1:34254").expect("Failed to send data");
```

```rust
let mut buf = [0; 1024];

let (amt, _) = socket.recv_from(&mut buf).expect("Failed to receive data"); println!("Received: {}", String::from_utf8_lossy(&buf[0..amt]));
}
```

This client sends a message to the UDP server and prints the response. ## 9.5 Error Handling

Rust is known for its strong type system and safety features, which extend to error handling in networking. Utilize the `Result` and `Option` types to manage potential errors gracefully and maintain control of your program's flow.

Example of Error Handling with TCP:

```rust
fn main() {

match TcpStream::connect("127.0.0.1:7878") { Ok(mut stream) => {

// Proceed to send/receive data

}

Err(e) => {

eprintln!("Could not connect to the server: {}", e);
```

```
}
}
}
```

9.6 Asynchronous Networking

For modern applications requiring high concurrency, asynchronous networking in Rust is made possible utilizing libraries like `tokio`. This allows you to handle multiple network connections without blocking threads, resulting in highly efficient applications. Below is a simple asynchronous TCP server example:

```rust
use tokio::net::{TcpListener, TcpStream};

use tokio::io::{AsyncReadExt, AsyncWriteExt};

#[tokio::main] async fn main() {

let            listener            = TcpListener::bind("127.0.0.1:7878").await.unwrap();
println!("Server listening on port 7878");

loop {

let (socket, _) = listener.accept().await.unwrap();
tokio::spawn(async move {

handle_client(socket).await;

});

}

}

async fn handle_client(mut socket: TcpStream) { let mut
```

```
buffer = [0; 1024];

while let Ok(size) = socket.read(&mut buffer).await { if
size          ==          0          {          break;          }
socket.write_all(&buffer[0..size]).await.unwrap();

}

}
```
` ` `

This code sets up a simple echo server using async programming patterns that let you manage multiple connections concurrently.

Networking in low-level Rust programming allows developers to tap into the power of system-level programming while benefiting from Rust's safety and concurrency features. Understanding how to utilize both TCP and UDP in Rust equips you with essential tools to build robust networked applications or embedded systems requiring efficient communication.

Building Network Protocols from Scratch

This chapter explores how to build network protocols from scratch using Rust, a systems programming language that offers memory safety, concurrency, and performance—ideal for developing low-level network applications.

Why Rust for Network Protocol Development?

Rust is designed for performance and safety, making it an excellent choice for developing network protocols:

Memory Safety: Rust's ownership model eliminates common bugs found in systems programming, such as null pointer dereferences and buffer overflows. This is especially important in network programming, where vulnerabilities can have critical implications.

Concurrency: Rust's abstractions make it easier to write concurrent code, facilitating the development of protocols that need to handle multiple connections simultaneously.

Performance: Rust produces highly optimized binaries that compete with C and C++. The zero-cost abstractions mean you can write high-level code without sacrificing performance.

Expressive Type System: Rust's type system helps ensure that errors are caught at compile time rather than at runtime. This is crucial for protocols where data integrity is paramount.

In this chapter, we will guide you through the process of creating a simple network protocol in Rust, specifically a custom echo protocol, where a client can send messages to a server and receive the same messages back.

5.1 Setting Up Your Development Environment

Before diving into the code, you'll need to set up your development environment. Ensure you have Rust installed on your system. You can install Rust via `rustup`, the Rust toolchain installer:

```bash
```

```
curl --proto '=https' --tlsv1.2 -sSf https://sh.rustup.rs | sh
```

After installation, make sure to keep Rust updated:

```bash
rustup update
```

We will also use the `tokio` library, a runtime for writing asynchronous applications in Rust, which is especially useful for network programming:

```bash
cargo add tokio
```

5.2 Designing the Echo Protocol

Before we implement our protocol, we must first define its basic structure. The echo protocol will consist of the following parts:

Client: A program that connects to the server, sends a message, and waits for a response.

Server: A program that listens for incoming connections, reads a received message, and sends the same message back to the client.

5.2.1 Protocol Messages

We will define a simple protocol where each message is just a string. The client will send a message, and the server will respond by sending the same string back.

5.2.2 Design Considerations

Error Handling: Network programming often

encounters unexpected situations. We must handle errors gracefully, ensuring that our application can recover or shutdown gracefully.

Concurrency: The server must handle multiple clients simultaneously. Rust's concurrency model will allow us to use asynchronous programming to manage this efficiently.

5.3 Implementing the Echo Server

Let's first implement the server. Create a new Rust project:

```bash
cargo new echo_server cd echo_server
```

Next, in the `Cargo.toml` file, add the following dependencies:

```toml
[dependencies]
tokio = { version = "1", features = ["full"] }
```

Now, we can create the server logic in the `src/main.rs` file:

```rust
use tokio::net::{TcpListener, TcpStream};
use tokio::io::{AsyncBufReadExt, AsyncWriteExt, BufReader}; use std::error::Error;
#[tokio::main]
async fn main() -> Result<(), Box<dyn Error>> {
```

```
let listener = TcpListener::bind("127.0.0.1:8080").await?;
println!("Server running on 127.0.0.1:8080");

loop {

let (socket, _) = listener.accept().await?;
tokio::spawn(async move {

handle_client(socket).await.unwrap();

});

}

}

async fn handle_client(mut socket: TcpStream) ->
Result<(), Box<dyn Error>> { let reader =
BufReader::new(&mut socket);

let mut lines = reader.lines();

while let Some(Ok(line)) = lines.next_line().await {
println!("Received: {}", line);
socket.write_all(line.as_bytes()).await?;

socket.write_all(b"\n").await?; // Send back the same line
followed by a newline

}

Ok(())

}
```
```

### Server Explanation

**TcpListener**: The server binds to a local address and listens for incoming connections.

**Handle Client**: Each accepted connection is handled

149
```

in a separate task. We read lines asynchronously from the client and send the same line back, appending a newline character.

5.4 Implementing the Echo Client

Now, let's create the client. In the root directory, create a new project:

```bash
cargo new echo_client cd echo_client
```

Update the `Cargo.toml` file similarly to the server's. Now, we can add the client logic in `src/main.rs`:

```rust
use tokio::net::TcpStream;

use tokio::io::{self, AsyncBufReadExt, AsyncWriteExt, BufReader}; use std::error::Error;

#[tokio::main]

async fn main() -> Result<(), Box<dyn Error>> {

let mut stream = TcpStream::connect("127.0.0.1:8080").await?; println!("Connected to the server.");

let stdin = io::stdin();

let reader = BufReader::new(stdin); let mut lines = reader.lines();

while let Some(Ok(line)) = lines.next_line().await { stream.write_all(line.as_bytes()).await?; stream.write_all(b"\n").await?; // Send the line with
```

newline

```
let mut buffer = String::new(); stream.read_line(&mut
buffer).await?;   println!("Received   from   server:   {}",
buffer.trim());
}
Ok(())
}
```

Client Explanation

TcpStream: The client connects to the server's address.

User Input: The client reads lines from standard input, sending them to the server and waiting to receive the echoed response.

5.5 Running the Application

To run the echo server, navigate to the `echo_server` folder and execute:

```bash
cargo run
```

In another terminal, navigate to the `echo_client` folder and run:

```bash
cargo run
```

You can now type messages in the client terminal, and the server will echo them back to you. ## 5.6 Conclusion

In this chapter, we have explored the fundamentals of

building a simple network protocol using Rust. We discussed Rust's advantages for network programming and provided a hands-on example of creating an echo server and client using asynchronous programming with the `tokio` library.

As you progress in your understanding, consider expanding on this example by implementing more complex protocols, adding features such as authentication, multiplexing connections, or introducing different types of message handling. The foundations laid in this chapter will serve you well as you venture deeper into network programming in Rust.

Rust Programming Language: [The official Rust book](https://doc.rust-lang.org/book/)

Tokio Documentation: [Tokio's official documentation](https://tokio.rs/) provides extensive resources on asynchronous programming in Rust.

Network Programming: For a broader perspective, refer to network programming books that cover the theoretical underpinnings of protocols and data transmission.

Implementing Socket APIs in Rust

One of its key strengths is its ability to handle concurrency and low-level system interactions. In this chapter, we will delve into implementing socket APIs using Rust, focusing on TCP and UDP protocols—two of the most common networking paradigms.

The chapter will cover:

An introduction to Rust's standard library support for sockets.

Establishing TCP connections using Rust.

Implementing a basic UDP client and server.

Handling errors and resource management.

Best practices and further considerations. ## Understanding Rust's Socket APIs

Rust provides low-level socket programming capabilities through the `std::net` module in its standard library. This module offers the essential types and methods needed to work with TCP and UDP sockets in a safe manner.

Key Types:

`TcpListener`: For creating a TCP server which can listen for incoming connections.

`TcpStream`: Represents a TCP connection between two machines.

`UdpSocket`: Used for sending and receiving messages in a connectionless protocol. ### Setting Up Your Rust Environment

Before we begin implementing our socket APIs, ensure that you have Rust installed on your machine. You can download it from the [official Rust website](https://www.rust-lang.org/). Once Rust is installed, create a new project:

```bash
cargo new rust_socket_example cd rust_socket_example
```

```
```

Now, let's explore TCP connections. ## Implementing TCP Connections ### Creating a TCP Server

First, we will implement a simple TCP server that can accept incoming connections. Create a new file called `tcp_server.rs` in the `src` directory:

```rust
use std::net::{TcpListener, TcpStream}; use std::io::{BufReader, BufRead, Write}; use std::thread;

fn handle_client(stream: TcpStream) {

let mut reader = BufReader::new(stream.try_clone().unwrap());

let mut buffer = String::new();

// Read client message

match reader.read_line(&mut buffer) { Ok(_) => {

println!("Received: {}", buffer);

// Echo the message back
stream.write_all(buffer.as_bytes()).unwrap();

},

Err(e) => eprintln!("Failed to read from client: {}", e),

}

}

fn main() {

let listener = TcpListener::bind("127.0.0.1:8080").expect("Could not
```

```
bind"); println!("Server running on 127.0.0.1:8080...");
for stream in listener.incoming() { match stream {
Ok(stream) => { thread::spawn(move || {
handle_client(stream);
});
},
Err(e) => eprintln!("Failed to accept connection: {}", e),
}
}
}
```

Explanation

TcpListener: This binds to the specified address and starts listening for connections.

handle_client: Each connection is handled in a separate thread. The server reads a line from the client and echoes it back.

Incoming Connection: The server loops over incoming connections and spawns a new thread for each client, enabling concurrent connections.

Creating a TCP Client

Next, let's create a TCP client to communicate with our server. Create another file called `tcp_client.rs`:

```rust
use std::net::TcpStream;
```

```rust
use std::io::{self, Write, BufReader, BufRead};

fn main() -> io::Result<()> {

    let mut stream = TcpStream::connect("127.0.0.1:8080")?;
    println!("Connected to the server!");

    let stdin = io::stdin();

    let reader = BufReader::new(stdin);


    for line in reader.lines() { let message = line?;

    stream.write_all(message.as_bytes())?; let mut buffer =
    String::new();      stream.read_line(&mut      buffer)?;
    println!("Server echoed: {}", buffer);

    }

    Ok(())

    }
```

Explanation

TcpStream: This is used to connect to the server.

Reading Input: The client reads from standard input and sends each line to the server, then waits for the echoed response.

Implementing UDP Sockets

Now that we've built a basic TCP communication system, let's explore UDP using a client-server model. Unlike TCP, which is connection-oriented, UDP is connectionless and faster.

Creating a UDP Server

Create a file called `udp_server.rs`:

```rust
use std::net::UdpSocket;

fn main() -> std::io::Result<()> {

let socket = UdpSocket::bind("127.0.0.1:8080")?;
println!("UDP server running on 127.0.0.1:8080...");

let mut buf = [0; 1024]; loop {

let (number_of_bytes, src) = socket.recv_from(&mut buf)?;         let         msg         =
String::from_utf8_lossy(&buf[..number_of_bytes]);
println!("Received from {}: {}", src, msg);

// Echo the message back socket.send_to(msg.as_bytes(), src)?;

}

}
```

Creating a UDP Client Similarly, create `udp_client.rs`:

```rust
use std::net::UdpSocket; use std::io::{self, Write};


fn main() -> std::io::Result<()> {

let socket = UdpSocket::bind("127.0.0.1:0")?; // Bind to a random free port println!("UDP client running...");

let stdin = io::stdin(); loop {
```

```rust
let mut input = String::new();

stdin.read_line(&mut input)?;

let result = socket.send_to(input.as_bytes(), "127.0.0.1:8080");

match result {
Ok(_size) => println!("Sent: {}", input.trim()),
Err(e) => eprintln!("Could not send: {}", e),
}
}
}
```

Error Handling and Resource Management

In both TCP and UDP implementations, we've used basic error handling via `expect` and `match` to handle failures.

A crucial concept in Rust's safety model is ownership, which automatically manages memory. When sockets go out of scope, Rust ensures that the resources are freed. Always strive to handle errors gracefully, ensuring your application doesn't crash unexpectedly.

Best Practices

Use Libraries: For more complex networking tasks, consider using libraries like `tokio` or `async-std` for asynchronous programming patterns.

Concurrency: Use Rust's concurrency features,

158

including threads and the `async`/`await` syntax, to improve performance in I/O bound applications.

Error Handling: Always handle potential errors to improve the robustness of your applications.

Testing: Rigorously test your networking code to handle various network conditions such as timeouts or unexpected disconnections.

By utilizing Rust's powerful standard library and adhering to best practices, you can create efficient, safe, and concurrent networking applications. As you advance, consider exploring asynchronous programming with Rust, allowing for even more robust and scalable networked applications.

Chapter 10: Security Features in Rust-Based Systems

Rust, a modern programming language designed with safety and performance in mind, offers unique features that help developers create secure applications. This chapter explores the security features inherent to Rust-based systems, examining how they contribute to mitigating common vulnerabilities and enhancing overall software security.

10.1 Memory Safety

One of Rust's most notable features is its rigorous approach to memory safety. Traditional programming languages like C and C++ often suffer from vulnerabilities related to memory management, such as buffer overflows, use-after-free errors, and null pointer dereferences. Rust addresses these issues through its ownership model combined with a strong type system.

10.1.1 Ownership and Borrowing

Rust's ownership model enforces strict rules about how memory is accessed and manipulated. Every value in Rust has a single owner, which ensures that resources are automatically cleaned up when they go out of scope. This eliminates many classes of memory-related vulnerabilities without requiring a garbage collector.

Additionally, Rust's borrowing mechanism allows developers to temporarily "borrow" values without transferring ownership. This enables safe concurrent access to data while ensuring that mutable and immutable references do not coexist, preventing data races.

10.1.2 Lifetimes

Lifetimes in Rust provide a way to track how long references to data are valid. By making explicit the scope of each reference, Rust helps prevent dangling pointers and ensures that data is not used beyond its intended lifetime. The compiler enforces these rules at compile-time, allowing developers to catch potential errors early in the development process.

10.2 Concurrency Safety

With the rise of multi-core processors, concurrent programming has become an essential aspect of software development. However, writing concurrent code safely remains a significant challenge. Rust's concurrency model is designed to prevent common pitfalls associated with multi-threading.

10.2.1 Fearless Concurrency

Rust promotes "fearless concurrency" through its ownership and type system. The compiler ensures that data races are impossible by enforcing strict rules regarding the sharing of data between threads. Immutable data can be shared freely across threads, while mutable data is restricted to a single thread at any given time.

10.2.2 Channels and Mutexes

Rust provides built-in abstractions for managing concurrency, such as channels for message passing and mutexes for locking shared resources. These primitives make it easier to write safe concurrent code without resorting to low-level synchronization primitives, reducing the likelihood of race conditions and deadlocks.

10.3 Type Safety

161

Type safety is a fundamental concept in programming languages that helps catch errors at compile time rather than runtime. Rust's strong static typing system ensures that variables must be explicitly declared and checked for compatibility.

10.3.1 Enums and Pattern Matching

Rust's enums and pattern matching capabilities allow developers to define types that can represent multiple variations, making it easier to model complex data structures safely. This feature enables exhaustive checking, meaning the compiler can verify that all possible cases are handled, reducing the risk of runtime errors.

10.3.2 Option and Result Types

Rust introduces the `Option` and `Result` types, which help deal with the absence of values and error handling in a type-safe manner. Instead of returning null or throwing exceptions (as seen in other languages), functions return `Option<T>` to indicate potential absence of a value or `Result<T, E>` to convey whether an operation succeeded or failed. This approach forces developers to handle these cases explicitly, significantly reducing the chances of null pointer exceptions or unhandled errors.

10.4 Secure Standard Libraries

Rust's standard libraries are designed with security in mind. By providing safe constructs for common tasks, such as file I/O, networking, and data manipulation, Rust helps developers avoid common pitfalls that lead to security vulnerabilities.

10.4.1 Safe APIs

Many APIs in Rust are designed to be safe by default. For

example, when handling potentially toxic input, such as user-entered data, Rust encourages the use of safe parsing functions that prevent buffer overflows and similar risks. These APIs abstract away many of the complexities of secure coding practices while still giving developers the control they need.

10.4.2 Community-Driven Security

The Rust community actively contributes to the language and ecosystem, emphasizing security in its libraries and tools. This communal focus fosters a culture of best practices and shared knowledge, leading to a continuously improving security landscape for Rust applications.

10.5 Tooling and Ecosystem

Rust's tooling ecosystem plays a crucial role in enhancing security. Tools like `cargo audit` can identify vulnerabilities in dependencies, ensuring that developers are aware of potential threats before their applications go into production. Similarly, Rust's extensive testing framework encourages developers to write comprehensive unit and integration tests, further enhancing software reliability.

10.5.1 Static Analysis

Rust's ownership model allows for static analysis tools to be highly effective. By analyzing code at compile time, these tools can catch potential security issues early in the development process, reducing the likelihood of defects in the final product.

10.5.2 Fuzzing and Instrumentation

Fuzz testing is an effective method for discovering security vulnerabilities. Rust supports integration with fuzzing tools that help identify edge cases and unexpected behaviors in code. Coupled with instrumentation, developers can detect and rectify security risks proactively.

By leveraging its memory safety, concurrency guarantees, strong typing, and a supportive ecosystem, developers can create robust, secure applications with confidence. Understanding and utilizing these features is crucial for anyone looking to build secure Rust-based systems, ensuring that software remains resilient against evolving threats in an increasingly complex digital world.

Leveraging Rust's Safety for Secure Systems

This chapter explores how Rust, a systems programming language designed with safety in mind, provides robust mechanisms to build secure systems effectively. We will delve into Rust's unique features—like its ownership model, type system, and concurrency support—and demonstrate how these elements contribute to developing secure applications.

The Importance of Security in Software Development

Software security is not just a goal; it is a fundamental requirement in software engineering. Vulnerabilities can lead to data breaches, loss of sensitive information, system downtime, and even financial losses.

Traditional programming languages such as C and C++ often expose developers to common pitfalls—such as buffer overflows and null pointer dereferences—that can be exploited by malicious actors. Rust addresses many of these vulnerabilities at the language level, thereby reducing the attack surface of the systems built with it.

Rust's Ownership Model ### Understanding Ownership

At the core of Rust's design is the ownership model, which governs how memory is managed. Rust enforces a set of rules that ensure memory safety without requiring a garbage collector. Each value in Rust has a single owner at any given time, and when the owner goes out of scope, the memory is automatically freed.

This model eliminates the risks associated with double-free errors and memory leaks, common culprits in insecure systems.

Borrowing and Lifetimes

Beyond ownership, Rust introduces the concepts of borrowing and lifetimes, offering more flexibility while maintaining safety. Borrowing enables developers to access data without taking ownership of it, allowing for both mutable and immutable references. Lifetimes are annotations that allow the compiler to ensure references are always valid, preventing dangling pointer issues.

By embracing ownership, borrowing, and lifetimes, Rust restricts the conditions under which memory can be accessed and modified, creating a secure environment for system development where unintentional memory corruption is virtually eliminated.

Type System and Safety ### Strong Typing

Rust's strong and static type system enhances reliability by catching errors at compile time rather than at runtime. By defining the types of data that are used, developers can avoid misusing them, which is a common source of vulnerabilities in other languages.

Pattern Matching

Rust's comprehensive pattern matching capabilities further enhance type safety, allowing developers to handle different data structures robustly. This is particularly useful in managing enums and data structures that can have multiple valid states. By requiring developers to handle all possible cases, Rust mitigates the risk of runtime errors and unexpected behavior in secure systems.

Concurrency Without Fear

Concurrency is essential in modern applications, but it often comes with a host of security issues, such as data races and deadlocks. Rust's approach to concurrency is based on the principle of ownership and borrowing, which makes it easier to write safe concurrent code.

Fearless Concurrency

Rust's type system ensures that data races are caught at compile time. For instance, if a variable is borrowed mutably, no other borrows (mutable or immutable) can coexist. This eliminates the classic pitfalls of concurrent programming, allowing developers to write performant and secure multi-threaded applications without the dread of introducing subtle bugs.

Leveraging Libraries and Frameworks

When building secure systems in Rust, developers can leverage numerous libraries and frameworks designed with security in mind. The Rust community has focused on creating libraries that encapsulate complex security protocols and features. Some notable libraries include:

Tokio: An asynchronous runtime that allows secure and efficient handling of I/O operations.

Actix: A web framework that emphasizes security and performance.

Serde: A framework for serializing and deserializing data securely.

Utilizing these libraries can accelerate the development of secure applications while adhering to Rust's safety guarantees.

Practical Secure System Development in Rust ### Case Study: Building a Secure Web Server

To demonstrate how Rust's features contribute to building secure systems, let's consider the task of developing a simple web server. In this project, we leverage crates like Actix and Tokio, adhering to Rust's safety principles throughout.

Setting Up Dependencies: We begin by specifying the required libraries in our Cargo.toml file. This includes Actix for the web framework and Tokio for handling asynchronous operations.

Defining Data Structures: We define our types and use Rust's enums to handle different request types securely. The ability to model request states ensures we account for every scenario, minimizing unexpected behaviors.

Error Handling: Rust's Result and Option types encourage explicit error handling, making the system robust against unexpected input. This way, we avoid crashes and potential security vulnerabilities from unhandled scenarios.

Concurrency Handling: Using async/await syntax, we build a concurrent server that handles multiple requests simultaneously without risk of data races. The compiler's checks ensure that all memory accesses are safe.

Testing and Validation: Finally, we implement comprehensive tests, another critical aspect of secure system development. Rust's testing framework allows us to systematically validate that our application behaves as expected.

As we have seen, Rust's design principles and features provide a powerful foundation for developing secure systems. By leveraging the ownership model, type system, and fearless concurrency paradigm, developers can eliminate common vulnerabilities that plague traditional programming languages. Furthermore, the Rust ecosystem offers an array of libraries and tools designed to streamline secure application development.

Writing Secure Bootloaders and Kernels

Bootloaders and kernels are the foundational layers of any operating system, and they are often the primary targets for attackers seeking to compromise system security. Consequently, writing secure bootloaders and kernels has become a critical area of focus in system programming.

Rust, a systems programming language known for its emphasis on safety and concurrency, presents a

168

compelling alternative to traditional languages like C and C++ for developing secure software. With its unique ownership model, strong type system, and adherence to best practices, Rust provides mechanisms that can significantly mitigate common security vulnerabilities. This chapter will delve into the principles and practices of writing secure bootloaders and kernels in Rust, examining key concepts, tools, and methodologies that contribute to enhanced system security.

Understanding Bootloaders and Kernels
What is a Bootloader?

A bootloader is a small program that initializes the system and loads the operating system kernel into memory. It is the first piece of code executed when a device is powered on. Its responsibilities include hardware initialization, loading the operating system, and transferring control to the kernel. Given its critical role in system startup, a compromised bootloader can jeopardize the entire system.

What is an Operating System Kernel?

The kernel is the core of an operating system, acting as an intermediary between the hardware and software. It manages system resources, provides essential services, and enforces security policies. The kernel operates in a privileged mode, making it a prime target for exploitation. Ensuring the kernel's security is vital for the overall security posture of the system.

The Case for Rust in System Programming
Memory Safety

One fundamental challenge in system programming is managing memory safely and efficiently. Traditional languages like C and C++ allow direct manipulation of memory, which can lead to vulnerabilities such as buffer overflows and null pointer dereferences. Rust's ownership model prevents these issues by enforcing strict rules about memory access and lifetime.

By leveraging Rust's features such as ownership, borrowing, and the type system, developers can encode their intentions more explicitly and avoid common pitfalls associated with memory management.

Concurrency

Concurrency is another aspect where Rust excels. In a multi-threaded environment, managing access to shared resources is critical. Rust's concurrency model ensures that data races are caught at compile time, promoting safer concurrent programming practices. This is particularly important in kernel development, where multiple threads may access shared memory, and ensuring the integrity of data structures is paramount.

A Growing Ecosystem

The Rust community has made significant strides in creating libraries and tools tailored for systems programming. Prominent projects such as `rust-std`, `no_std`, and `embedded Rust` facilitate the development of low-level software while maintaining Rust's safety guarantees. These libraries provide essential abstractions and functionalities needed to implement bootloaders and kernels.

Key Concepts in Writing Secure Bootloaders and Kernels ### 1. Code Integrity

Code integrity ensures that the software executed is

exactly what was intended and has not been tampered with. Techniques such as cryptographic signing should be employed to verify the integrity of the bootloader and kernel binaries. Rust's support for embedded cryptographic libraries enables developers to implement secure signing and verification protocols.

2. Minimal Surface Area

Following the principle of least privilege, both bootloaders and kernels should have a minimal codebase to reduce the attack surface. Writing clean, purposeful code helps prevent unintended vulnerabilities. Rust's emphasis on modular design and type safety allows developers to create smaller and more maintainable codebases.

3. Secure Error Handling

Robust error handling is vital to maintaining system security. In Rust, the use of the `Result` and `Option` types provides a clear mechanism for handling errors. Employing these types helps prevent runtime panics that could lead to leaks of sensitive information or unhandled states that could be exploited.

4. Secure Boot

Secure Boot is a security standard that aims to ensure that a device only loads trusted software during the boot process. Implementing Secure Boot in a Rust-based bootloader involves verifying the signatures of the bootloader and the kernel against a known trusted key. Rust's ecosystem supports modern cryptographic libraries that facilitate the implementation of this security measure effectively.

5. System Call Filtering

When developing a kernel, implementing a robust system call interface is crucial. System call filtering allows the restriction of user-space interactions with kernel resources, significantly reducing potential vectors for attacks. Rust's strong typing can help enforce strict APIs for system calls, ensuring only valid and expected interactions occur.

Best Practices for Writing Secure Rust Bootloaders and Kernels

Keep Dependencies to a Minimum: Use only necessary libraries to reduce potential vulnerabilities.

Regular Code Audits: Conduct thorough code reviews to identify and fix security flaws.

Follow the Principle of Least Privilege: Ensure components run with the minimal privilege necessary.

Utilize Rust Tools: Leverage tools like `cargo audit` to check for vulnerabilities in dependencies.

Employ Testing and Fuzzing: Write unit tests and integrate fuzz testing frameworks to discover edge cases and bugs.

Stay Updated: Keep abreast of the latest vulnerabilities, tooling, and best practices within the Rust ecosystem.

With its emphasis on memory safety, concurrency, and effective error handling, Rust allows developers to write robust software that mitigates many common vulnerabilities encountered in systems programming.

Chapter 11: Debugging and Testing Low-Level Rust Code

Rust's strong emphasis on safety, ownership, and concurrency gives developers powerful tools at their disposal for identifying and resolving issues, but understanding how to effectively leverage these tools in a low-level context is crucial. In this chapter, we will explore various techniques and best practices for debugging and testing low-level Rust code.

11.1 Understanding Debugging in Rust

Debugging is the process of identifying and resolving errors or issues in code. In the Rust ecosystem, developers benefit from a rich set of debugging tools and techniques. At the low level, when working with system resources, the complexity of debugging often increases due to factors like memory management, concurrent processes, and direct hardware interactions.

Rust's compiler is one of the primary debugging aids. The borrow checker ensures that many common classes of bugs, such as data races and null pointer dereferences, are caught at compile time. Still, bugs can and do occur at runtime, particularly in low-level code.

11.1.1 Built-in Debugging Features

Compile-Time Checks: The Rust compiler provides strict compile-time checks that help prevent common errors. Make use of these checks by adhering to Rust's ownership and borrowing rules.

Debug Assertions: Rust provides the `debug_assert!` macro, which allows you to check conditions during

173

debugging builds. These assertions can help catch logic errors early.

Logging: The `log` crate provides a standardized way to log information in Rust applications. For low-level programming, effective logging can provide insights into the flow of execution and the state of the system.

Debugging Levels: Use `cargo build --profile=debug` to compile your program with debugging information. This allows you to inspect your code with tools such as `gdb`, `lldb`, or IDE-integrated debuggers.

11.2 Debugging Tools for Low-Level Code

When dealing with low-level Rust code, utilizing various external debugging tools can significantly aid in diagnosing issues.

11.2.1 GDB and LLDB

GDB (GNU Debugger) and LLDB (the LLVM Debugger) are invaluable tools for debugging compiled Rust binaries. They allow you to set breakpoints, step through code, inspect variables, and analyze the call stack.

Tips for Using GDB/LLDB:

Compile your code with debug symbols using the `--release` flag only for final builds; for debugging, rely on the debug profile.

Familiarize yourself with commands like `break`, `next`, `continue`, and `print` to facilitate effective debugging sessions.

11.2.2 Valgrind

Valgrind is a tool for memory debugging, memory leak detection, and profiling. It is especially useful when dealing with raw pointers and memory allocation in Rust.

Use command `valgrind ./target/debug/your_program` to analyze memory usage and locate leaks or illegal memory accesses.

11.2.3 Rust-Specific Tools

Rust Analyzer: A language server that provides features like code completion, in-line errors, and references tracking. It can be particularly helpful in low-level contexts to understand how various parts of the code interact.

Miri: An interpreter for Rust's mid-level intermediate representation (MIR). It performs checks on code at a higher level and can help find undefined behavior.

11.3 Testing Strategies for Low-Level Rust Code

High-quality, reliable code is built upon a solid foundation of testing. Low-level code often interacts directly with hardware, so testing needs to be meticulous.

11.3.1 Unit Testing

Unit tests check individual components in isolation. Use Rust's built-in test framework for creating unit tests in your codebase.

- Use the `#[cfg(test)]` attribute to include tests in your modules:

```rust
#[cfg(test)] mod tests {
use super::*;

#[test]
fn test_function() {
assert_eq!(your_function(), expected_value);
}
}
```

11.3.2 Integration Testing

Integration tests ensure that components work together as expected. Place integration tests in the `tests` directory at the root of your project.

Use command `cargo test` to run both unit and integration tests. Consider integrating hardware mockups or simulation environments to test hardware interactions.

11.3.3 Property Testing

Property testing (also known as generative testing) involves specifying properties that all valid inputs should satisfy. The `proptest` crate is a popular choice for this in Rust.

It is particularly useful for fuzz testing low-level code, as it can automatically generate inputs based on specified constraints.

11.4 Best Practices

Keep It Simple: Write simple, modular low-level

components. This makes testing and debugging easier.

Document Assumptions: Clearly document any assumptions regarding the hardware or environment your code interacts with — this can save time during debugging.

Automate Testing: Use Continuous Integration (CI) pipelines to automate tests for your low-level Rust code, ensuring consistent feedback on code changes.

Use Assertions: Use assertions liberally to catch bugs early in the development process—`assert!` can provide quick feedback while developing low-level features.

By understanding debugging techniques, utilizing available tools, and adopting robust testing strategies, developers can ensure that their low-level Rust applications are both reliable and maintainable. As you continue your journey with Rust, remember that these practices will enhance not only the quality of your code but also your overall development experience.

Debugging Techniques for Rust Kernels

Rust, with its strong emphasis on safety and concurrency, introduces unique debugging techniques that can significantly enhance the process of identifying and resolving issues within kernel development. This chapter aims to provide a comprehensive overview of debugging techniques specifically tailored for Rust kernels, enabling developers to improve their debugging skills and write more robust systems code.

1. Understanding Rust's Safety Guarantees

Rust's design ensures memory safety through its ownership model, which eliminates data races and dangling pointers at compile time. This foundation allows developers to focus on higher-level logic rather than low-level memory management. However, this does not mean that Rust applications, including kernels, are free from bugs. Understanding Rust's safety guarantees is the first step in effective debugging. Familiarize yourself with concepts such as borrowing, lifetimes, and ownership, as they can help you trace back issues in your kernel code.

2. Leveraging Compiler Warnings

The Rust compiler (rustc) is not just a tool to convert your code to machine language; it also serves as an incredibly powerful ally in debugging. By enabling a higher level of warnings, developers can catch potential issues early in the development process. Use the following flags when compiling your kernel code:

```bash
cargo build --release --warn
```

Common warnings to look out for include unused variables, unreachable code, and mutable borrow problems. Addressing these warnings proactively can prevent many runtime errors.

3. Utilizing the Rust Debugger: GDB and LLDB

For deeper inspection of running programs, using a debugger like GDB or LLDB is crucial. Rust provides good support for both of these debuggers. GDB has integrated support for Rust's data structures, which makes it easier to inspect them during runtime.

To setup debugging with GDB:

Compile your Rust kernel in debug mode (the default mode when running `cargo build`).

Start GDB with the generated binary.

```bash
gdb target/debug/my_kernel
```

Use GDB commands to set breakpoints, watchpoints, and inspect memory.

Key commands include:

`break <function>`: Set a breakpoint at the start of the specified function.

`run`: Start the program.

`bt`: Display the call stack.

`print <variable>`: Inspect the value of a variable.

4. Logging for Diagnostics

In kernel development, using logging effectively can simplify the debugging process. Rust's `log` crate provides a flexible logging framework that you can integrate into your kernel. Utilize different log levels (`error!`, `warn!`, `info!`, `debug!`, `trace!`) to output useful information.

Here's a simple example of how to set up logging in your

kernel:

```rust
use log::{info, warn};

fn init() {

info!("Kernel initialized."); warn!("This is a warning message.");

}

fn main() {

// Initializing logger here, typically with a suitable backend for kernel. init();

}

```

To gather logs, make sure that you configure an appropriate logger and define where the logs should be stored or sent for analysis.

5. Runtime Analysis Tools

Tools such as `valgrind` can be invaluable for locating memory-related issues in your kernel. Although Rust's ownership model mitigates many of these problems, using `valgrind` alongside your development can uncover elusive bugs.

For example, run your kernel under `valgrind`:

```bash
valgrind ./target/debug/my_kernel
```

Keep an eye out for common issues like memory leaks and

180

invalid accesses. ### 6. Fuzz Testing

Fuzz testing is an effective technique for exposing vulnerabilities in your kernel. Tools like `cargo-fuzz` can be used to randomly generate inputs and scenarios for your kernel code, allowing you to observe how your code behaves under unexpected conditions.

To set up fuzz testing:

Add `cargo-fuzz` to your project:

```bash
cargo install cargo-fuzz
```

Create a fuzz target that invokes parts of your kernel code.

Start the fuzzing session:

```bash
cargo fuzz start <target_name>
```

Monitor the results and refine your input strategies based on the findings to increase the coverage of edge cases.

7. Fail Fast: Panics and Assertions

In Rust, `panic!` is the go-to mechanism for indicating unrecoverable errors. Leveraging assertions during the development can catch errors at runtime effectively. Use `assert!`, `assert_eq!`, and `assert_ne!` to enforce invariants within your kernel code. This helps in identifying problems early and can significantly simplify debugging.

Example:

```rust
fn divide(a: usize, b: usize) -> usize { assert!(b != 0,
"Cannot divide by zero."); a / b
}
```

8. Integrating Continuous Testing

Finally, integrating continuous testing and automated CI/CD pipelines can streamline the debugging process. Each time a change is made to your kernel, automatically trigger a series of tests that validate its integrity and functionality. Use Rust testing frameworks to write unit and integration tests for your functions.

A minimal test can be structured as follows:

```rust
#[cfg(test)] mod tests {
use super::*;
#[test]
fn test_divide() { assert_eq!(divide(10, 2), 5);
}
}
```

By understanding the language's features, leveraging logging, utilizing debuggers, employing fuzz testing, and adopting effective testing strategies, developers can significantly reduce the time spent debugging and improve the overall quality of their kernel code.

Testing Rust Systems Code for Reliability

While Rust's robust type system and ownership model offer considerable advantages in preventing common programming errors, test-driven development remains an essential practice for ensuring the reliability and correctness of systems code. This chapter aims to outline best practices, tools, and strategies for testing Rust systems code, emphasizing the importance of building robust applications that maintain reliability and performance in a demanding environment.

1. Understanding the Need for Testing

Before diving into the practical aspects of testing, it's essential to recognize why testing is critical for Rust systems code. Systems programming often involves managing resources, handling concurrency, and interacting with hardware components—all of which can introduce subtle bugs that are difficult to detect. These bugs can lead to catastrophic failures or security vulnerabilities in production systems.

1.1 Types of Testing

There are several types of testing that are particularly relevant for systems code:

Unit Testing: Focuses on individual components or functions to ensure they perform as expected in isolation.

Integration Testing: Examines how different modules work together, ensuring that data flows correctly between components.

Property-Based Testing: Generalizes the idea of unit

testing by checking whether certain properties hold true for a range of inputs, using libraries like `quickcheck`.

Fuzz Testing: Involves feeding unexpected inputs to the program to uncover vulnerabilities.

Benchmarking: Measures the performance of specific functions to ensure the system meets performance criteria.

Understanding these types of testing allows developers to select appropriate strategies tailored to their project's requirements.

2. Writing Tests in Rust

Rust provides built-in support for testing. The standard library includes a testing framework that allows developers to write unit tests, integration tests, and documentation tests seamlessly. Here's how to get started:

2.1 Unit Tests

Unit tests are typically written in the same file as the code they test, within a module annotated with

`#[cfg(test)]`. This annotation ensures that the module is compiled only for testing purposes. Below is an example of a simple unit test:

```rust
// src/lib.rs
pub fn add(a: i32, b: i32) -> i32 { a + b
}


#[cfg(test)] mod tests {
```

```
use super::*;
#[test]
fn test_add() { assert_eq!(add(2, 3), 5);
assert_eq!(add(-1, 1), 0);
}
}
```

2.2 Integration Tests

Integration tests are placed in the `tests` directory. Each file in this directory is compiled as a separate crate, allowing you to test your library in a more realistic context. An example of an integration test could look like this:

```rust
// tests/integration_test.rs
use my_crate::add; #[test]
fn test_add_integration() { assert_eq!(add(10, 5), 15);
}
```

2.3 Documentation Tests

Rust also allows you to write tests within comments in your documentation. This ensures that examples are always up to date and gives users confidence in the code's behavior. Here's how to add documentation tests:

```rust
```

```
/// Adds two numbers together.
///
/// # Examples
/// ```
/// let sum = add(2, 3);
/// assert_eq!(sum, 5);
/// ```
pub fn add(a: i32, b: i32) -> i32 { a + b
}
```
```

## 3. Leveraging Rust's Features for Testing

Rust includes a variety of features that enhance the testing process: ### 3.1 Assertions and Panic

The `assert!`, `assert_eq!`, and `assert_ne!` macros are at the core of writing effective tests in Rust. They provide meaningful error messages and leverage Rust's ability to ensure safety by panicking when conditions aren't met.

### 3.2 Test Filtering

During development, you may want to run only a specific subset of tests. Rust provides flags such as `--test` and `test-filter` to allow focused testing, helping to accelerate the testing process.

### 3.3 Handling Asynchronous Code

As systems programming often involves asynchronous operations, Rust's `async` testing support is crucial. The `tokio` or `async-std` libraries can be used in conjunction
```

with Rust's built-in test framework to handle async tests effectively.

4. Going Beyond Basic Testing

While the built-in testing functionalities are valuable, robust systems code often necessitates a more comprehensive approach, including:

4.1 Continuous Integration (CI)

Implementing CI pipelines that run tests automatically upon code changes helps maintain code quality. Tools such as GitHub Actions, Travis CI, and CircleCI can be configured to run Rust tests, ensuring that all contributions are checked against the test suite.

4.2 Code Coverage

Measuring code coverage allows you to identify untested parts of your codebase. Tools like `tarpaulin` or

`grcov` can be integrated into your testing workflow to generate coverage reports. ### 4.3 Fuzz Testing and Security Checks

Fuzz testing tools like `cargo-fuzz` enable you to identify edge-case bugs by randomly feeding input data into your program, effectively testing the application's resilience. Additionally, integrating security analysis tools helps in identifying potential vulnerabilities.

Testing Rust systems code is not merely an optional practice; it is essential for building reliable systems that can operate confidently in a complex environment. By employing a variety of testing strategies—from unit tests and integration tests to property-based testing—developers can ensure that their code is well-structured, secure, and performant. Coupling these practices with continuous integration and automated tests leads to a robust development workflow that significantly contributes to the overall reliability of systems written in Rust.

Conclusion

In this Book, we embarked on an exciting journey through the Rust programming language and its transformative potential for operating system development. As we explored the intricacies of Rust, it became increasingly evident that its unique features—such as ownership, borrowing, and a strong emphasis on memory safety—are not just advantageous, but essential for building modern, efficient, and secure operating systems.

We delved into key concepts such as memory management, concurrency, and low-level system programming, highlighting how Rust enables developers to tackle the challenges that have historically plagued OS design. By leveraging Rust's capabilities, we can eliminate entire classes of bugs at compile time, reducing the likelihood of runtime failures and security vulnerabilities. This shift in focus toward safety and performance allows us to create more reliable and resilient systems that can meet the demands of today's distributed and high-concurrency environments.

Moreover, we examined practical applications of Rust in real-world operating system components and projects. From kernel development to user-space applications, Rust proves to be a formidable ally in the quest for performance and security. As more developers embrace Rust, we can anticipate a significant evolution in the landscape of operating systems—one that prioritizes not just speed but also safety and simplicity.

As you stand on the brink of developing your own secure and high-performance operating systems using Rust, remember that the journey doesn't end here. The Rust community is vibrant and ever-evolving, with an abundance of resources, libraries, and frameworks to support your endeavors. Engaging with this community can provide invaluable insights and drive innovation as we collectively explore the vast potential of Rust in operating systems.

Biography

Jeff Stuart is a visionary writer and seasoned web developer with a passion for crafting dynamic and user-centric web applications. With years of hands-on experience in the tech industry, Jeff has mastered the art of problem-solving through code, specializing in Rust programming and cutting-edge web technologies. His expertise lies in creating efficient, scalable, and secure solutions that push the boundaries of what web applications can achieve.

As a lifelong learner and tech enthusiast, Jeff thrives on exploring the ever-evolving landscape of programming languages and frameworks. When he's not immersed in writing code or brainstorming innovative ideas, you'll find him sharing his knowledge through inspiring content that empowers others to unlock their full potential in the digital world.

Beyond his professional pursuits, Jeff enjoys exploring the art of minimalist design, reading thought-provoking books on technology and philosophy, and hiking to recharge his creative energies. His unwavering dedication to excellence and his belief in the transformative power of technology shine through in every page of his work, making this book a compelling guide for anyone eager to master the art of Rust programming and web development.

Glossary: Rust Programming Language for Operating Systems

1. **Allocator**

A component responsible for managing memory allocation in a program. In the context of operating systems, an allocator ensures that memory is efficiently distributed among various processes and handles memory deallocation.

2. **async / await**

Syntax in Rust that enables asynchronous programming, allowing tasks to run concurrently without blocking the main thread. This is particularly useful in OS development for managing multiple I/O operations without stalling system processes.

3. **Crate**

A package of Rust code. Each crate can be a library or an executable, and Rust's package manager, Cargo, manages these crates and their dependencies, facilitating modular system design.

4. **Cargo**

Rust's package manager and build system. Cargo simplifies dependency management, project compilation, and package publishing, making it easier to build complex systems, including operating systems.

5. **Concurrency**

The ability to run multiple computations simultaneously. Rust's ownership model provides mechanisms to write concurrent code safely and efficiently, which is vital in an operating system for handling multiple processes.

6. **Debugging**

The process of identifying and fixing bugs or issues within a program's code. Rust's compiler is designed to provide detailed error messages, helping developers debug their systems effectively.

7. **Error Handling**

Rust emphasizes safe error handling through the Result and Option types, allowing developers to manage failures gracefully. This is especially critical in operating systems where failures can lead to system instability.

8. **FreeRTOS**

A real-time operating system kernel designed for microcontrollers. Rust can be used to develop applications that run on such environments due to its performance-oriented design and safety features.

9. **Mutability**

In Rust, variables are immutable by default. Mutability

must be explicitly declared, promoting functional programming principles and creating safer code, particularly important in OS-level code management.

10. **Ownership**

A central concept in Rust that dictates how memory is managed. Each value in Rust has a single owner, which helps eliminate issues like dangling pointers and memory leaks, crucial for stable and secure operating systems.

11. **Borrowing**

The act of temporarily using a value without taking ownership. Rust allows mutable and immutable borrowing, which enables flexible memory access patterns—important in systems programming where resources are limited.

12. **Lifetime**

A mechanism that Rust uses to track how long references to data are valid. Lifetimes help prevent dangling references, ensuring memory safety, a vital aspect of OS reliability.

13. **No Standard Library (#![no_std])**

A compilation directive that allows developers to work without Rust's standard library, which is essential in operating systems where limited resources and direct hardware interactions are required.

14. **Kernel**

The core component of an operating system that manages system resources, hardware, and communication between software and hardware. Rust can be used to develop kernels with improved safety and performance characteristics.

15. **Thread Safety**

A measure of ensuring that shared data is accessed by multiple threads without causing data races. Rust's ownership and borrowing principles aid in ensuring thread safety, which is critical in multi-threaded OS environments.

16. **Unsafe Code**

Code blocks that allow for low-level memory manipulation and interactions with the underlying hardware. While powerful, unsafe code comes with inherent risks, and Rust provides mechanisms to isolate and minimize its use.

17. **Static Analysis**

The analysis of code without executing it to find potential errors. Rust's compiler performs extensive static analysis, allowing developers to catch bugs early in the development process, which is essential for operating system reliability.

18. **Zero-Cost Abstractions**

A principle wherein higher-level programming constructs do not incur additional runtime overhead. Rust leverages zero-cost abstractions to enable writing efficient, high-level code without sacrificing performance, crucial for OS development.

www.ingramcontent.com/pod-product-compliance
Lightning Source LLC
LaVergne TN
LVHW051332050326
832903LV00031B/3492